MOM
AT WAR

A Story of Courage and Love Born of Loss

by Todd Parnell

PFLP Publishing, L. L. C.
P.O. Box 3180
Springfield, MO 65808-3180
417-844-1388
toddparnell@pflp-publishing.com

Library of Congress Control Number: 2005908260

ISBN: 0-9772173-0-2

Printed and bound in the United States of America by Jostens Publishing, Topeka, KA.

Page Composition and Cover Design: Jeff Jasper

Editing: Dr. Frank Reuter

Proofreading: Melissa Parnell, Betty Parnell and Kim Chism Jasper

Printing Consultant: Tom Shields

Website Design: Jason Stanley, Stanley Design Group

Cover portrait: Original charcoal sketch of Mom done by a GI shortly after V-E Day.

Foreward

I have known Jean Elizabeth Hogg Rayl Parnell longer than any other living human being ... and that's the only reason her son, Todd, asked me to write the foreword of his marvelous book called MOM AT WAR.

Jean and I started primary grades together and my research shows that I truly have known her longer than any other living human. Abandoning all modesty I must admit that there are other reasons for Todd's investing me with such an honor:

1) I am most sensitive and very perceptive, a truly great judge of human character.

2) I know a pretty girl when I see one ... and Jean was acclaimed class Beauty Queen from grades one through 12 in Springfield's public schools.

It was in the third grade that I realized there was a difference between boys and girls. Jean was not only the prettiest but also the tallest boy or girl. She was taller than I, still is, but has never mentioned this to me.

At age 13, I was sent, over my protests, to a ballroom dancing class tutored by a talented woman named Anne Louise Horn-Bostel. This took place in a ballroom atop a downtown hotel of six stories. This was to keep adolescent boys from shinnying out the bathroom windows and escaping.

For the first time, Jean's height was a disadvantage. All teen-age boys of that day used a diabolically contrived super oil called 'brilliantine' to tame their locks.

Jean always wore a pristine white shirt waist with a handsome long skirt. God, she was beautiful.

Trouble was, each boy-partner stained that shirt waist at somewhere around bosom height. You could see the various marks depending on how tall each partner was. I'm sorry to say that I was low man on Jean's brilliantine totem.

✦　✦　✦　✦

Jean's first husband was a handsome young man named John Rayl. He was a fraternity brother of mine at Drury University. He was not very popular. He was too tall, too handsome, too hail-fellow well-met. Also, his steady girl was Jean. It's no wonder that most of us were not overly fond of the lucky stiff.

He went to West Point Military Academy; Jean went off to Arkansas University. Then, World War II intervened.

Jean and John dropped their program paths ... and got married. They wanted as much time as possible together. They had a few precious months before John shipped out as a second lieutenant in a combat company.

The second lieutenant who wrote Jean the consolation note told her how much the enlisted men respected John ... what a fine officer he was ... how the artillery barrage that killed him instantly on their landing in Sicily was no respecter of truly good men.

After Jean used up a lifetime of tears, she opened her eyes, sat down and did some serious thinking. She was not the kind of person to live in a pity-party the rest of her life. Then she sat down with her mother and father and tried to tell them exactly how she felt.

She was able to put into words how strongly she felt about getting personally involved in the great cause for which her husband had given his life. She had cried all the tears she had. She wanted to DO something.

After much thought, she had decided to join the American Red Cross.

Her parents respected her decision, realizing how very much she wanted to do this and understanding her deep emotions, and wished her Godspeed.

✦　✦　✦　✦

Like the good daughter she had been brought up to be, and like the meticulous and systematic person she was, she wrote them regularly ... interesting letters ... about the young women she was serving with ... the new experiences ... travel abroad ... the romance of making and dispensing doughnuts to our young service men and how much they appreciated seeing American girls driving Hillman trucks through the rough roads of Europe ... too near the front lines too often.

At the same time, she kept a diary in which she wrote faithfully, including some things she might not have put in her letters for fear of worrying her parents. In that journal, she mentioned Springfield folks she met in England or France --- including one Ben Parnell, of whom you will read more.

Not long ago, Todd Parnell, Jean's oldest son, was browsing through ancient artifacts and found the box of letters, which her parents had cherished and carefully saved ... he also found her diary. He spent a lot of time reading and enjoying her excellent writings ... then comparing and dovetailing the letters and the diary.

Then, he began his labor of love ... he wrote MOM AT WAR.

I told Todd about four years ago that I was impatient for him to retire from banking and start writing full time. He is one of the finest yet to be published writers it has been my fortune to read. He just retired and fearlessly I'll predict you will greatly enjoy this outstanding book. It's about love.

Bill Cantrell
Lt. Col. USMC (ret.)

FRONT DE MER

EUROPE NORD-OUEST

au 2.000.000ᵉ

MEER-GRENZE
E U R O P A
NORD-WEST

PRIX NET : 18 Francs

COLLECTION BLONDEL LA ROUGERY

Table of Contents

Foreward   3

Acknowledgements   6

Prologue   8

Chapter 1   Loss   10

Chapter 2   Before   12

Chapter 3   The Box and the Book   14

Chapter 4   Basic Training   20

Chapter 5   Over There   28

Chapter 6   #3 Elliot Street   33

Chapter 7   Hammered in Heerlen   49

Chapter 8   New Year's at the Bulge   56

Chapter 9   Crossing the Rhine   66

Chapter 10   POWs and V.E.   81

Chapter 11   Winding Down   94

Chapter 12   Ever After   112

Postscript   116

Timeline   119

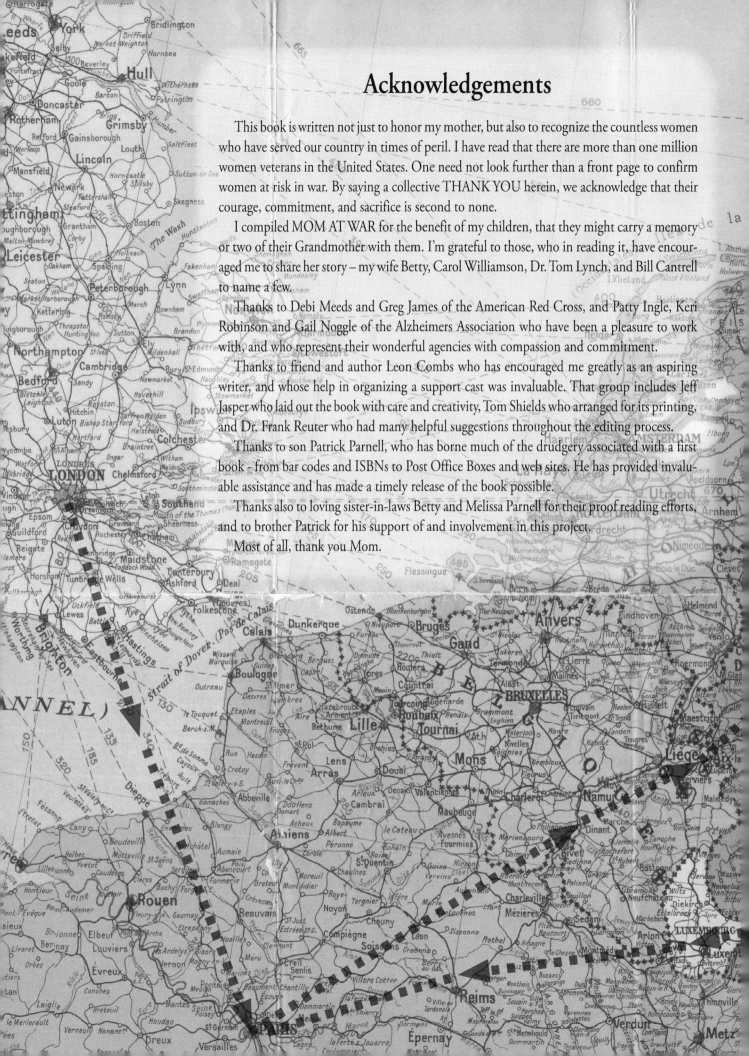

Acknowledgements

This book is written not just to honor my mother, but also to recognize the countless women who have served our country in times of peril. I have read that there are more than one million women veterans in the United States. One need not look further than a front page to confirm women at risk in war. By saying a collective THANK YOU herein, we acknowledge that their courage, commitment, and sacrifice is second to none.

I compiled MOM AT WAR for the benefit of my children, that they might carry a memory or two of their Grandmother with them. I'm grateful to those, who in reading it, have encouraged me to share her story – my wife Betty, Carol Williamson, Dr. Tom Lynch, and Bill Cantrell to name a few.

Thanks to Debi Meeds and Greg James of the American Red Cross, and Patty Ingle, Keri Robinson and Gail Noggle of the Alzheimers Association who have been a pleasure to work with, and who represent their wonderful agencies with compassion and commitment.

Thanks to friend and author Leon Combs who has encouraged me greatly as an aspiring writer, and whose help in organizing a support cast was invaluable. That group includes Jeff Jasper who laid out the book with care and creativity, Tom Shields who arranged for its printing, and Dr. Frank Reuter who had many helpful suggestions throughout the editing process.

Thanks to son Patrick Parnell, who has borne much of the drudgery associated with a first book - from bar codes and ISBNs to Post Office Boxes and web sites. He has provided invaluable assistance and has made a timely release of the book possible.

Thanks also to loving sister-in-laws Betty and Melissa Parnell for their proof reading efforts, and to brother Patrick for his support of and involvement in this project.

Most of all, thank you Mom.

Prologue

She stood straight and tall tonight, November 4, 2000 – almost at attention.

Fifty-six years earlier, she had been bouncing across Northern Europe at the wheel of a two and a half ton Hillman truck, supporting lead soldiers headed toward Aachen, Germany and the Battle of the Bulge, helping to reclaim the higher ground for humanity.

Tonight, leaning on her 81st year, she could only sing about it. That is what she does

best these days. That, and love humankind with warm gestures and embracing words of vague familiarity – "best friends" with most, known or not, memory slipping slowly into oblivion.

"WORLD WAR II MEMORIAL"
November 4th, 2000
Featuring Several
Big Band Acts
6:30 p.m.
Show time
Hosted by:
Nicholas W. Inman & Theresa Petry of KOLR 10
Sponsors: Wal-Mart, Jubilee Theater, Webster Co. Opry
5:30 p.m.
Dinner Served

World War II
Memorial
Fundraising
USO Performance

Hosted by: Nicholas W.
Inman and Tom Dye

Marshfield, Missouri – everyone here focused on the past this election eve for the future. The crowd is older, calmer, quieter than most. Some smile, some doze. The occasion is to gather funds for a World War II Memorial in Washington, D.C., some 1000 miles and a full culture away, through reminiscence, songs of then. The building creaks with each note, from the National Anthem with many hands on hearts, to "America, the Beautiful," to "Boogie Woogie Bugle Boy."

And then, they are up. The honorary host, a retired TV weatherman of their generation, provides an introduction that includes the observation that he could listen to them all evening. They – Them – The Tritones: Mom, and friends Marge Petit and Ginny Reynolds, singing together for 20 years, singing of life before the War to end all wars.

They begin with "Sentimental Journey," voices merged in the perfect harmony of time, practice and friendship. Marge arranges and plays it her way, with subtle changes in rhythm and pace. Old. Professional. Touching. The crowd quickly awakens and embraces them with boisterous appreciation. They slow to "Dream… when you're feeling blue ." Inspiring. Uplifting. Comforting. Eyes glisten around me, as do mine.

Then age and poor lighting attempt to steal the show. Marge gets lost halfway through her arrangement of "Chicago," and begins to mutter. Mom quickly shuts down. Ginny picks up the pieces by suggesting that they start this one over. Mom quips, "Maybe we'd better quit while we're ahead," not immediately aware that everyone in the house has heard and chuckled. The crowd roars its encouragement to the brave old ladies on stage.

Throughout the performance, no eyes gleam brighter than those of Patricia Jean Parnell – granddaughter, namesake. It would be the only time she sees her Grandmother Jean in the bright lights. She is here because my wife insisted, made it happen. Patricia Jean will remember.

It ends too soon for me, probably a good thing since Patricia is desperate for a toilet.

Mom seems strangely anxious to finish. Like the War, she has had enough.

Mom spent July 1944 through October 1945 at war. She fought authorities and her mother for permission to sign up. She fought grief and loss. She fought for the United States of America, behind front lines, serving and supporting the soldiers who slogged through Europe. She served with bravery and honor, and as a snapshot of a time and place beyond most of her gender's generational experience. She fought and won.

Most of what follows was drawn from her failing memory, a tattered scrapbook, and an ammo box of letters to and from her parents. At one point as we were digging through her remembrances, she commented that it was the "first time I've gone over all this with anyone since my parents." Thus my need to get it down on paper – it is a tale of courage worth preserving.

CHAPTER 1

Loss

This story begins as most important things do, with an end.

Dear Mrs. Rayl:

Though the letter was first opened by her mother at their house on North Benton Street in Springfield, Missouri, the news was delivered to her by her father. As she sat filling out forms at the Standard Appliance Store, a business repossessed by her father's finance company, the back door opened. She remembers her father looking "white as paper." "I have very bad news," he said. "Johnny has been killed." It had happened on August 2, 1943, in the Mediterranean theatre. Johnny was her husband of less than two years.

Dear Mrs. Rayl:

The author of the devastating letter was Samuel P. Knight, Jr. The date in the top right hand corner: Sunday, August 29. The return address: Somewhere in Sicily.

Dear Mrs. Rayl:
I have just finished a hard task, that of signing my name under the notation, Addressee Reported Deceased, on all your letters to John. It seemed rather cold and curt to just say that and nothing more. I am married myself and I know the suffering caused by the death of some one who is so close that he is an integral part of you. I just wanted you to know that his memory is with us all here in K Company.

John was one of the finest officers in the regiment, and whenever his name is mentioned among his men, you hear phrases like, 'coolest man I ever saw under fire'…. I heard these myself when I took over his platoon on August 3 after he had been killed. He was doing what he always did, taking care of his men with cool courage, trying to get them out of an area that was being shelled, exposing himself to the enemy while his men got away. More than half of his platoon had escaped when it came. He never knew what it was, and he died fighting. His actions in the face of the enemy showed his bravery in the highest light, and it was due to his actions that the enemy guns were located and silenced by our own, thus enabling the whole Battalion to advance to its objective. His actions truly reflect great credit on himself and the military service …

We miss him and his soft Missouri accent …. He was very religious about writing you, and if we stopped for half an hour he would have a letter all written to you and ready to mail. From what he had told us you must be a very wonderful woman … John Rayl died because he believed that our country and our way of living was worth protecting … I know that nothing I say can ease the terrible pain that is yours now.

Samuel Knight was certainly right about that.

CHAPTER 2

Before

Mom was born on December 30, 1919, the second and last daughter of Jessie Warden and Jesse Wyman Hogg. She was named Elizabeth Jean Hogg, Elizabeth after an aunt, and Jean, after who knows? She believes she was born in a house on Dollison Street, although she can't today pinpoint location.

The Hoggs had migrated from St. Louis County just after the Civil War. They had owned a large farm that adjoined the Hibler farm on what are now the grounds of Bellereive Country Club. The Hoggs and Hiblers intermarried, with Jess Hogg and Pamilia Hibler moving to Springfield and siring J. Wyman among others. Jess Hogg

was in the finance business, a path his son chose as well.

J. Wyman was blessed with a booming baritone voice and a stalwart religious faith, which he put to use in the formation of First and Calvary Church, also on Dollison Street. Jesse Warden was the daughter of a brilliant, alcoholic doctor, lost her mother at childbirth, and was raised by her grandmother. She struck me as aloof, smart, and a bit withdrawn. They were respected and active in the Springfield community.

Mom remembers John Rayl from age 14 and from First and Calvary where he attended. His father was a doctor. They also lived on Benton Street. John

J. Wyman and Jessie Hogg with Mary and Baby Jean (above)

Jess and Pamilia (Hibler) Hogg with grandkids - Jean in middle

attended Wentworth Academy prior to being admitted to the U. S. Military Academy at West Point. Mom remembers winning a beauty contest as Johnny's date at Wentworth her senior year in high school. Actor Fred McMurray picked her from a picture.

When Johnny went to West Point, Mom went to University of Arkansas. Ironically, it was there that she had her first date with my dad, who was a traveling secretary for Lambda Chi Alpha fraternity. She returned to Springfield and Drury College, just up the street on N. Benton, and for reasons I'm unclear about started her sophomore year there. Likewise, Johnny returned from West Point after two years. Again, I'm not sure why.

They were married on November 21, 1941. Johnny enlisted in the Army and shortly thereafter, they began to crisscross the country. First, it was Ft. Lewis, Washington. Mom remembers her shock on learning of the Japanese attack on Pearl Harbor as they rode the train to Ft. Lewis. Then it was back to Georgia, then Carmel, California, for three months, and finally orders to report to Virginia for assignment to the Grand Armada, which was shipping out for the African Invasion. She recalls waving goodbye to Johnny for the last time in 1942. He was dead in Sicily a year later. She was the first among her friends and acquaintances to lose a husband.

Johnny's body was not returned for burial until 1947, long after Mom had married my father, and when I was four months old. Dad insisted on accompanying her to the memorial service at First and Calvary and interment in a north-side cemetery.

That fall of 1943 Mom took her grief to Ruth Luster's house on Walnut Street, where she joined several other ladies in sewing hats and masks to forward to GIs for warmth.

One day, Ruth approached Mom with something "new and different." The American Red Cross needs people overseas the flyer said. Mom took it home.

When she shared it with her parents, Jessie shook her head NO. J. Wyman read it, and simply said "If she wants to, I'm all for it, and will see that she gets to do it." He approached Dr. Findlay at Drury College for help. "Can you get Jean an interview with the Red Cross in

Kansas City?" Mom and J. Wyman were soon on the train for K.C. for not one, but seven, interviews. The problem was a fundamental one: eligibility guidelines mandated age 25. Mom was 24.

Her plea was simple and heartfelt:

"I became a war widow at 23, and am tired of sitting around feeling sorry for myself."

"I want to get out of self and do something for someone else."

"I'll make the best Red Cross girl you have ever had."

Somehow she carried the day. Whether it was maturity, determination, credibility, emotion or all of the above, she was accepted. The age requirement was waived, one of only three waivers she was ever aware of. On June 2, 1944, she put her grief on a shelf and left Springfield for Washington, D.C., training, and forwarding to the European Theatre. Mom was going to war.

CHAPTER 3

The Box and the Book

The box and the book are what remain of Mom's fifteen months at war.

I hoist the heavy old wooden ammo box to the dining room table. The handles on each end are of rope, now frayed. They are attached to the box by a 2" x 4" block of wood, mounted with four tarnished screws. The rope gives, but doesn't break. The top of the box reads "Patronenkast 88," with a capital "B" underneath. On the side is "HEERES-Munition." "Heer" evidently means Army in German. The serial number is gzz194. All very orderly, very German. I question what it means, but only for a moment. This is not about a box, but that which lies inside: a glimpse back at my mom, 1944-45, some 56 years past.

The black metal latch pops effortlessly. My hands shake slightly as I crack the lid. Hinges swing open the wooden top. Not a sound after half a century. Again, very German.

It is time to go through Mom's stuff. I am two cups of coffee into the morning and am about to delve deeper into her life than ever before. Not sure why I waited until now, Memorial Day, 2001.

The underside of the lid reads "German Ammunition Box" in Mom's fluid hand, and in the center imprinted on the wood several German descriptives. Judging from the numbers, I can only assume length or type of shells.

The contents are stacked neatly inside: letters, pamphlets, souvenir post-cards, a coin purse and money belt, a long slender wooden pipe with tiny brass mouthpiece and bowl, a large three piece pottery pipe with tiny

tamp, a button or two, and a light brown fake leather fold-over wallet.

The wallet looks to be stuffed with significance, so I decide to start there. I lift it gently from its spot in the corner. The top of a man's head peers out from behind a flap. He shows dark, wavy hair, shaved close on the sides. Kind of looks like my college son wears his today,

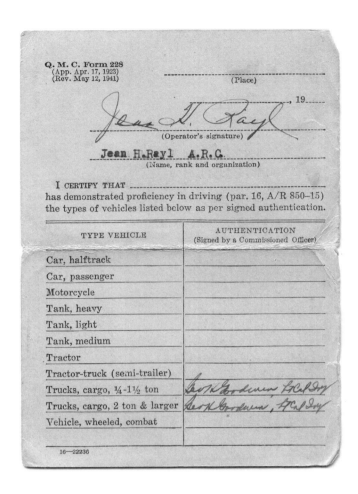

Q. M. C. Form 228
(App. Apr. 17, 1923)
(Rev. May 12, 1941)

_____
(Place)
_____, 19____

_____
(Operator's signature)

Jean H. Rayl A.R.C.
(Name, rank and organization)

I CERTIFY THAT _____
has demonstrated proficiency in driving (par. 16, A/R 850-15)
the types of vehicles listed below as per signed authentication.

TYPE VEHICLE	AUTHENTICATION (Signed by a Commissioned Officer)
Car, halftrack	
Car, passenger	
Motorcycle	
Tank, heavy	
Tank, light	
Tank, medium	
Tractor	
Tractor-truck (semi-trailer)	
Trucks, cargo, ¼–1½ ton	Geo H. Goodwin, Lt Col Inf
Trucks, cargo, 2 ton & larger	Geo H. Goodwin, Lt Col Inf
Vehicle, wheeled, combat	

16—22236

January 1942, in Tacoma, Washington, shortly before he shipped off to death.

More pictures are nestled beneath of Mom in front of the Dixie Queen Clubmobile, and in other war settings. There is a Folies Bergere ticket #01761 followed by her vaccination records (four typhus shots in 12 months), and a blank "Warshipticket." Finally, a prayer card from her father, "I Pray for You" by Olive Mercer:

> I pray for you while you are far away…
> I pray for you because you're dear to me…
> I ask that you'll safely return to me
> When peace is won and ours is victory.
>
> "Your Dad"

So simple. So patriotic. Folded inside the prayer card is a tiny caricature, probably done by her sister Mary who had an artistic flair, featuring her uniformed photo on a desk, with her beloved dog Chappie sitting in front crying dog tears. Why these particular pictures, messages, and mementos in her war wallet, the one she carried everywhere with her?

The flip side of the wallet contains her Motor Vehicle Operators Permit designating "Trucks, cargo, ¼ - 1½ ton" and "Trucks, cargo, 2 ton & larger" as her vehicles of choice. There are more prayer cards, a note in German, a clothing ration card, a meal card, a room assignment (M-41) from the Princes Gate, a few receipts and addresses. Many stories here I'm sure, most to be left untold. I slip the wallet back into the box. I am beginning to feel like an intruder.

Next up is a package, two thick manila envelopes, folded and stapled. Inside are buttons and insignia, from her uniform I guess. ARC means American Red Cross no doubt.

There are many pictures, ones that didn't make the scrapbook cut, incredibly beautiful postcards from England, France, Belgium, and Germany, as well as maps, guidebooks, "The Overseas Woman," a propaganda piece from the good guys that featured articles

a far cry from mine of a similar age in the late '60s.

I pull out the folded plastic shield and stare at the man who could have been some iteration of my father I suppose. I would have definitely looked different, for he shares no resemblance to my dad, except for rather large ears. Maybe it was the haircut. Both were handsome men in their own way. So this was Johnny – John Rayl. I don't recall seeing a picture of him before. The back reads "Sunday, Nov. 3, 1940, Thayer Hall, West Point," almost a year before they wed. Why would she choose this picture of him to carry to war? I thumb through other small photos of him, same date – Cadet Chapel, hazing a plebe, and then in full dress uniform,

on everything from "Fashions of War" to "Hitler's Women…help kill American soldiers." Lots to read here, but later.

I lift the "Full Grain, Horse Hide, Cordovan" money belt from the box. The ripped zipper reveals her name and address – Jean H. Rayl,

American Red Cross, 930 H St., Wash., (13), D.C. – and a bundle of wadded currency. I find shilling and pound notes from England. Then, a paper parade of her journey – French Francs, Belgian and Luxembourg Francs, Nederland Guldens, and finally German Marks by the millions. Reichsbanknote, Eine Million Mark, 1,000,000 read one. Another, Landesbank, 1,000,000, Provinz Hannover, dated 9 August, 1923. My mom, the millionaire. Also, some really strange ones mixed in at random:

•tiny Oriental (Japanese?) notes in denominations of 10 and 50 somethings, some worn, some almost crisp
•DWA ZLOTE, from BANK EMISYJNYW POLSCE, denominated 2, crumpled, with a fully scarved, farm girl smiling from the wrinkles
•BANCO DO BRASIL,1 - something, with "Short Snorter" handwritten in ink at the top. Brazil? Short Snorter? It is autographed by several soldiers , often with dates and places.

"North Ireland, 7/6/44, E.B. Terrill, Jr."
"Denmark, July '44", name beyond reading.
"Ed Hadley, Edwina Russell, Bill Brown," no dates.
"Lt. Ben A. Parnell, Dec 20, 1943, Chinatown, Washington, D.C."

Almost like a chain letter, with Mom as the recipient who didn't pass it along.

The one that will stick in my mind is a 5 Mark Reichsbank Note issued in Berlin, August, 1942, with a large, arrogant, young Aryan face staring stonily from the corner. After all, this is what that awful war

was about.

A small "Manual of Information for American Red Cross Personnel in Great Britain and Western Europe" catches my eye. It specifies "Uniform and Equipment" for male and female personnel. Mom was limited to 2 towels, 1 sweater, and 2 suits of heavy underwear among other items. All this to get she and her comrades through a European winter? It's true when they say that my generation doesn't have a clue about what hers went through in WWII. I take more than that on a three-day float trip.

The manual lays out rules of "postal censorship," and addresses personal funds, the composition of a Club-mobile Unit and Group, personal hygiene, including a list for "female personnel" to include 1 brush, I mirror, and of course, cigarettes and 1 lighter. It concludes with "Casualty Announcements" (how Mom's parents would be informed if they lost her), and an organizational chart for the American Red Cross in Great Britain and Europe. The rules of life for Mom during her year at war, condensed to ten pages.

Underneath her Red Cross Manual, a diary, beginning with Friday, June 2nd, 1944, in Mom's beautiful handwriting. The last entry, Saturday, September 16, 1944, as she prepared to depart Southern England for the Continent. Perhaps I'll start with this.

Finally, the mother lode – stacks and stacks of letters, rubber-banded together, untouched for 50 years. I am struck by the numbers. Almost every letter has a number on it, at least through #78. It looked like my Grandfather's writing. Most appeared to be from her

= RED CROSS DIARY =
= 1944 =

Fri- June (2)nd - I left
Springfield tonight
for Wash to take my
Red Cross training
course. Gladys, Edward
& Jeanette put me on
the train.

Sat. June (3)rd Arrived
in St. Louis this
morning. Had lunch
& a ricky nice visit
with Martha Johner.
She put me on the
1:15 train this aft.
& I'm on my way
again

Sun. June (4)th Today I
met a girl on the
train who is on
her way to Wash. to
take the same course
I am. Her name is
Dorothy Fitzpatrick
from Jeff. City. We

and tell you how glad that we are that you are with us.

What a brazen blankety-blank this Private Smerin. He had never met Mom, and was attempting a seduction on the spot! He went on with a weak attempt at humor relating to their billeting in a maternity hospital.

I am sure that it does not add to your peace of mind to know that you are not only now dodging bombs but also must occupy all your spare time with wondering about what your family and friends will think about you so far from home and in a maternity hospital…,

It closes with a macho boast.

We are now over the hump and well on our way to finishing the job that the other guy started.

Certainly hope she had the pleasure of dumping a hot cup of coffee in his crotch. Amazing how easily a Mother's son is offended at harmless male drivel even a half century past.

Letter #78 is dated May 31, 1945. The letters continue beyond that one, more than 100 in all, from June 5, 1944, Washington, D.C., to September 19, 1945, Paris, France; nearly one letter every four days. I've yet to read one in full, except "Miss Delightful." Despite the volume, I find myself starting to wonder if I will really find much here, given War Zone censorship of the day. The only

to them, with a few from friends mixed in. It was as if they knew that someone, sometime would care.

One that carries neither number nor date is from Private Charles Smerin. It is addressed to "Miss Delightful, new member, C Group." I feel the color creeping into my face. Should I open this one, or let it ride? Just how personal am I prepared to get in this look back at my mother?

I open the tri-fold slowly:

My Dear Miss Delightful,

Since we have not had a formal introduction, I had to use this informal introduction, and since you will probably be whisked away nightly by some lucky officer soon, I must take advantage of this opportunity to talk to you

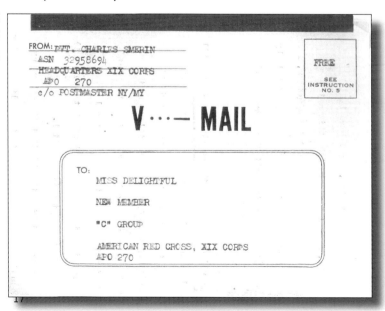

Group – history, itinerary, dispatches:

"Aachen, January 20, 1945
Clubmobile Group C fought the Battle of the
Bulge in Aachen. We are proud of the fact that
we moved ahead instead of backward in the
hectic days following the German breakthrough
in the Ardennes …"

Mom was in Group C, and there it was in bold headlines:

Red Cross Girls Fight Winter Do-Nut
Campaign in Aachen.

I run my fingers over a set of "dog tags" attached to a page by safety pin. They are made of cheap metal, her name punched through just short of breaking:

Rayl, Jean H
ARC 43666 T44 B

My mom, a number in the war of all numbers: 400,000 plus Americans dead, almost 700,000 wounded or maimed, countless others tragically scarred. And, the Jews, the Russians, the Asians, the Germans, the Brits, the Europeans – talk about numbers – the tragedy of

ship of the day. The only way to find out is one letter at a time. I will begin here, and with the diary. After I get my bearings, I will frame the discussion with her scrapbook. It too begins in Washington, at least the pictures do: Graduation, June 19, 1944.

Before the pictures are pages and pages about C

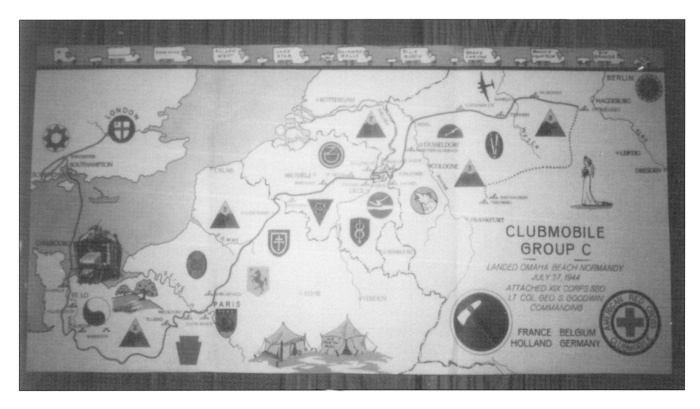

it all, and of all war. The metal tag is clipped to a solid metal chain that hung around her neck, often next to her heart, for fifteen months. I suppose they shipped these home if you were killed, for your loved ones to reverently caress, as I am doing now. Sobering.

Her scrapbook ends with a reunion picture, no date, but from her face and hair style, I would guess late '60s - early '70s, maybe a 25th anniversary meeting of Club-mobile Group C, maybe about the time I was bitterly protesting one of my generation being shot down in an anti-war protest at Kent State. Her smiling face belies the poison of those days. She wears her old uniform comfortably, and likely still could today.

Between beginning and end are the pictures: soldiers, ruins, celebrities, brave ladies, dancing in the streets, donut trucks, Germans, historical markers, most identified in her sweeping writing stroke.

There is history here – personalized, up-close, real. But there is more. I feel it when I look into the young dark eyes staring back from stale pages. There is wonder, even magic, born of tragedy, played out on an all too human stage, ending in triumph. Good over evil, beginnings over ends, women as equals, partners in service and in victory.

Repeating myself, I know. Yet, it keeps sticking in my mind, the serious voice that I only used to hear when I was in trouble – "I'll make the best Red Cross girl you have ever had." I have no doubt that she did.

CHAPTER 4

Basic Training

No more fitting name than **"CO-EDS THREE,"** could be chosen for this charming trio. They're Drury students, who formed their musical group just for fun, but clicked in radio when they auditioned at KGBX. Left to right they're Annabelle Heard, Martha Gilbert, and Jean Hogg. Their arrangements are done by accompanist Charlotte Wood.

RED CROSS DIARY - 1944
FRI – JUNE 2
I left Springfield tonight for Washington to take my Red Cross training course.

This is how she began her story. I read through her diary and letters from Washington, and found them short, precise, orderly. There is a calmness to them that belied her victory in just being there. Her words are much better than mine, as I try to place myself in her space and time.

SAT – JUNE 3
Arrived in St.Louis this morning. Had lunch

and a very nice visit with Martha Johnson. She put me on the train this afternoon, and I am on my way once again.

Time moves in funny circles. Martha Johnson was one of her singing buddies from before the war. Martha Johnson's son, Dr. Jeff, now sits on the Board of Directors of the bank I recently helped found.

MON – JUNE 5
This morning we reported at American University for registration and further instruction on our two week course.

And from a letter of the same date, The Lafayette Hotel:

Dearest Folks,

I am now writing this letter on a stack of suitcases – the only available space at present in our crowded little quarters. There are four of us living in one little room, but it's plenty of fun. They're all such swell girls….from all parts of the country….Colorado, Washington, Iowa…. This week our lectures will be from 9:30-5:00, with time off for meals. We'll cover the history and background of R.C. this week….Next week we'll receive personal training depending on the type work we have been chosen to do – a week from Saturday is graduation with full dress uniforms and parade. It'll be a long, hard climb before that though.

All my love, Jeannie Bug

There was a certain naivety to it all, not unlike a young nation that was about to lose the same.

TUES – JUNE 6
Today is D-Day and Washington is one big uproar. We had classes as scheduled, with 15 min. out for prayer service for all of our boys in the invasion.

So short, so simple, so telling. Today the "uproar" would likely be about violating separation of church and state, praying on government premises and time.

The headline of the June 6, 2001, Springfield News-Leader observes: VETER-ANS AND THEIR TALES RAPIDLY FADING AWAY. Fifty-seven years after "the" D-Day, 1,100 World War II veterans are dying daily, far fewer than in those early days of retribution, far more than I imagined now. After all, Mom and Dad are still here, fighting their final battles – her memory, his Parkinson's. Fifty-seven years ago they were both in Washington.

WED – JUNE 7
I had dinner tonight with Ben at the Water-gate Inn.

Ben, as in Parnell, as in my Dad to be – both from the Missouri Ozarks, both claiming the other chased them around the world. This is the first of a litany of chance encounters from Washington to London to Paris that resulted in, among other things, my brother Patrick and me.

And, then again, a week later:

WED – JUNE 14
Ben took me to the Statler tonight for dinner. We went dancing at the Shoreham on the terrace. It was great fun.

SAT – JUNE 17
We graduated today, and received our assignments for extension work – I'm to report to Ft. Belvoir, Va. I'm to commute for two weeks. I called home tonight for the first time. It was so good to hear the folks again I forgot myself and talked almost 10 minutes. It was certainly well worth it and more just to hear them again.

WED – JUNE 28
Moved this morning to the Que Street Club. It is quite a comedown.

She elaborated in a letter from the same date:

Your letters were certainly a morale booster. They couldn't have come at a better time. Here's why! Last night around 10:00 we received notice to move from the Lafayette to the Que Street Club. It was bad enough to have to move, but the 'hole' we're moving into is terrific! I was in a terrible 'storm' for a while, but have things under control now.... You don't need to worry about my diet mother – you wouldn't know your daughter's appetite. I have my egg for breakfast and milk at least once and sometimes twice a day. I almost like the stuff now. We figure we won't always be able to get these luxuries. I'm getting plenty of everything but sleep – they say we're going to have to get used to not having much of that anyway. I feel wonderful in spite of it. I'm convinced you can get used to anything – especially in this work. I love it though. I only hope it won't be long before we get our real chance… We never know what's going to happen to us from one day to the next. This is what makes it so enjoyable – I love it more all the time. I guess I'd better bring this thing to a close for now – Looks as though I've spent most of the time writing about myself – how dull! I'll try to do better next time…

MON – JULY 3
Today we reported to American University. I was put on a committee to plan a year's program for an overseas Club. I know we're just marking time until "clearance."

WED – JULY 5
I called the folks again tonight. It's probably the last chance I'll have to talk to them.

Last chance sounds so final – doubt if she even thought about that as she wrote it down.

THURS – JULY 6
Today was "clearance." We were quite interested to learn we're to have 'winter issue' which means either England or France.

I guess she really had no idea where she was to be posted until that moment.

FRI – JULY 7
Clearance continued. More and more red tape.

Some things never change.

SAT – JULY 8
We will be 'alerted' from now until we reach our destination.

What Mom was not 'alerted' to was the fact that she would be having me three years to the day later. Should have re-upped Mom!

SUN – JULY 9
This morning we took our footlockers and duffel bags to the station. This afternoon we reported

to the station in full pack. There are 138 of us. We're divided into 6 groups with group and section leaders. I'm in group 5. From now on we will be regimented in this manner until we reach our destination.

There is that word again – destination. She had no clue as to hers apart from the winter pack. Having never been to war, I didn't until just now have a sense of the vast uncertainty she and the others faced. Uncertainty about destination, uncertainty about whether she would return, uncertainty about what the next day would bring, uncertainty about how one will react to fire and death. A soldier, in this case Red Cross volunteer, was totally at the mercy and direction of the one above her, and the one above him, and on and on. That has never happened in my adult life, as I could always choose another path if I didn't like the one I was on. They call personal choice desertion in war. Her life was totally beyond her control. At least she didn't have to face uncertainty about whether what she was doing was right – another difference in perspective.

We marched on the train in this fashion. It was rather warm with full packs which consist of:
1) musette bag
2) gas mask
3) belt with first aid kit and canteen

4) mess kit
5) helmet
6) raincoat
We arrived in New York at Penn Station around 9:30 this evening. We were met by the N.Y. Motor Corps Unit with police escort. We were driven directly to the St. George Hotel in Brooklyn. This is where we'll stay until we embark.

MON – JULY 10
We had our first meeting. From now on we're under the 'Military.' We cannot contact anyone or tell anything. It's certainly a temptation to call home. The 'FBI' is on our trail, so I guess I won't.

Paranoia, or good old Presbyterian guilt?

TUES – JULY 11
Another meeting today. We were given the day off while the first part of the alphabet were partially cleared...Tonight we went to the radio play "You Can't Take It With You" at the Music Hall.

WED – JULY 12
Today was our day for 'partial clearance.' The last half of the alphabet marched to the arsenal in formation. We were given a lecture on gas and proper means of protecting against it. We were given gas masks impregnate. Tomorrow we will be tested for the real thing.

THURS – JULY 13
Again we marched to the arsenal in formation. We were given another lecture on gas and then the final test. Our first trip to the gas chamber was with our masks already on. It wasn't bad except that tear gas is very irritating to the skin. Our next trip was quite to the contrary. We entered the chamber with our masks off, and it was up to us to get them on. There was some blistered skin and watery eyes before we got through. Tonight, we were 'alerted' after 7:00. Our suitcases were picked up leaving us with nothing but our musette bags and equipment.

A letter dated same added little, but did carry the "U.S.ARMY EXAMINER" tag for the first time, and showed taped evidence of tampering.

FRI – JULY 14
Today we all marched over to the Arsenal for our final physical exams. That physical was the biggest farce yet – nothing but a look in our throats and our skin for rash.

We were alerted this evening at 5:30. At 7:30 we had our final meeting before leaving in field pack. At 9:30 we were marched very quietly down the fire escape into a very dark alley where trucks were waiting for us. We were then driven down all the back streets in Brooklyn and Manhattan to our dock (Grace Line). We were then lined up inside in alphabetical order once again. The New York [word illegible] was there to serve us lemonade and donuts while we waited (in full pack) to embark. We moved by numbers (marked on our helmets) from there on. My number is 108. It was a great thrill to walk up the gangplank onto the Queen Elizabeth tonight. I was assigned to cabin M-41 with five other girls. They're a swell bunch of girls and I know that we're going to have a wonderful trip across together. We retired to our bunks, six mighty weary females."

The secrecy of their departure routine was in striking contrast to what I expected. Soldiers and support sneaking off under cover of night, rather than with a proper heroes and heroines send off. The next several entries provided answers, as did the news just this week (June 2001) that a German submarine's remains were discovered in the Gulf of Mexico, just 40 miles from the mouth of the Mississippi River. The enemy within forty miles of the homeland. It makes sense they took every precaution.

SAT – JULY 15
This was our first day aboard ship. When we arose this AM, we were still in N.Y. Harbor, much to our disappointment. We're on the 4th call for our two meals a day. We had breakfast at 10:30, at 11:15 – "emergency muster." Three blows on the claxton is our signal for this. With life preservers on we rush to the sports deck and remain there until the "all clear." The first half of the alphabet goes to the starboard side, the last half to the port side. This will be our routine until we reach our destination. Our leisure time can be spent in 3 places – our cabin, the lounge, or the sports deck. We took in all three this afternoon. We pulled out of N.Y. Harbor around 2:00 this afternoon – everyone was ordered below. We did wave goodbye to N.Y. and "Mother Liberty" through our port holes as we left. It was one of the biggest thrills I've ever had. Our first day out wasn't that rough. We had dinner at 8:00 and went up on deck for another airing before black-out time at 9:00 when everyone is ordered below. We spent the

evening in the lounge playing cards and talking to the officers until 11:15. All lights must be out and everyone must be in bed by 12:00. We moved our watches up an hour.

SUN – JULY 16
Today we arose at 9:00 A.M. – I had a very refreshing stroll on deck before breakfast. At 11:15 we had our "emergency muster." Spent the rest of the day on deck in the sun. The sun was very hot which made me think we're going south.

MON – JULY 17
We arose at the usual time this morning after a very hot night in our stuffy cabin. We learned that we had passed through the Bahamas – no wonder it's been so warm. After breakfast and "emergency muster," we had a meeting in the lounge to discuss the dos and don'ts aboard ship. From now on our life preservers "water wings" are to be carried with us at all times.

TUES – JULY 18
Arose this morning at usual time after a very hot night. Had breakfast – 'kippered herring' this time. After the usual emergency muster we had our first life boat drill – it went as follows: all of the GI's and lower ranking officers are lined up on the main deck. We line up last with Generals, Cols, and Majors. It was a little embarrassing to walk down there in front of all those men in our sweaters and slacks. This is all done in such a manner so that we'll be the first off in case of emergency. I was very much against this - these men are far more important than we are and should be rescued first. I also forgot to mention that no one below a Major is allowed on the Sports Deck. There were two Generals on our boat so we really "hobnobbed" with the brass. We spent the afternoon on the deck while the poor GI's sweat it out down below in their close quarters. Tonight the boat was very rough due to zig-zagging – there were a lot of seasick people.

Glasgow Cathedral

WED – JULY 19
We spent a very rough night zig-zagging. This is the most dangerous part of the trip due to submarines. We have been unescorted for the last few hours and will be for some time. We can't even radio at this point. It's much cooler today and probably will be from now on. We were warned to have our musette bags packed and canteens filled for an emergency drill during the night.

THURS – JULY 20
Nothing happened last night – we didn't have our drill. I slept with my shoes on – some of the girls slept fully clothed…Today we put on a variety show for the boys. I was unable to participate due to laryngitis. It was a very good show – we have a lot of talent in this group. This was our last night in the lounge. We land tomorrow in Scotland and most of them [soldiers] are pulling out. Everyone restocked at the ship's store – it'll probably be our last chance to buy American goods for some time. I've never seen such a supply – we bought Hershey bars by the box.

FRI – JULY 21
We saw land this morning for the first time in 6 days – we were so excited we could hardly eat. We passed through the Firth of Clyde, which gave us a great opportunity to see Ireland. The little houses and towns along the coast are so quaint and cute. The scenery was even still more beautiful as we got closer to Scotland. The landscape differs from ours. There are very few trees on the hills and mountains, which allows you to see greater distance. The little farms are so neat – each one looks to be surrounded by hedges. We anchored early this afternoon. We spent the afternoon on deck watching the troops move out. After supper, we spent the evening packing.

SAT – JULY 22
After an early breakfast we returned to our cabins. We lined up with full packs in alpha-

26

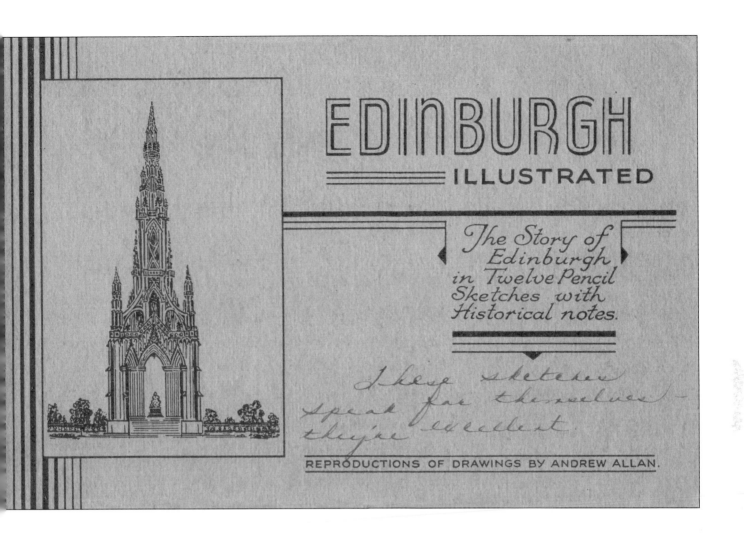

EDINBURGH

ILLUSTRATED

The Story of
Edinburgh
in Twelve Pencil
Sketches with
Historical notes.

These sketches
speak for themselves —
they're excellent.

REPRODUCTIONS OF DRAWINGS BY ANDREW ALLAN.

betical order and marched off the boat onto a barge. About 45 minutes later we set foot on Greenock, Scotland. While waiting for our train to leave the station, we were served coffee and donuts by the Red Cross. We then started our journey to London via Glasgow and Edinburgh....

Thus it was: Mom setting foot on foreign soil for

the first time in her short life, less than a year after losing her husband to the war she was about to enter. I confess to being struck by the dispassionate tone of her record. A few breaths of emotion leaked out, but not many. Where was she hiding her grief, her fear? Was it simply not allowed a woman of her generation and circumstance? Was it her Presbyterian heritage and upbringing? Would it show later?

CHAPTER 5

Over There

"Jean H. Rayl, daughter of J. Wyman Hogg, 1125 Benton Ave, Springfield, Mo., has arrived in England to serve the armed forces as an American Red Cross staff assistant. Until her Red Cross appointment, Mrs. Rayl was employed by the Standard Appliance Company. She attended Springfield Senior High School, Drury College, and the University of Arkansas."

Thus read the ARC formal press release forwarded to "Greene County" as scrawled in the corner of the onion paper copy. Mom was now official. No doubt a few hearts leapt and a few eyes leaked when they read the word in the Springfield *News-Leader*, for her story of loss was widely known about town. Not sure why it only referred to her father – just the times I guess. From Greenock, Scotland through Glasgow and Edinburgh, her train rumbled overnight to London, and a world at war.

SUN, July 23
This morning we arrived in London amid buzz bombs and blackouts. We were loaded onto trucks at the station and driven to Prince's Gardens. After breakfast and registering we all went to bed very tired people. We were given a room with a skylight on the very top of the building – good target…

MON, July 24
Final clearance at Hans Crescent Club. Had a very close call this afternoon with a bomb. Motor cut out directly overhead but it glided fortunately. Given choice of branch we wanted. I was certainly thrilled to get Clubmobile – 50 of us get it.

In August 1943, there was reportedly only one "Clubmobiler" from Missouri. One year later, as mentioned

KAK230 10 SER=WUX WASHINGTON DC 25 626P

J WYMAN HOGG=

:1125 BENTON AVE SPRINGFIELD MO=

1944 JUL 25 PM 6 10

:HAPPY TO REPORT SAFE ARRIVAL JEAN RAYL IN GREAT BRITAIN=

NUTTALL ARC.

RAYL NUTTALL.

THE COMPANY WILL APPRECIATE SUGGESTIONS FROM ITS PATRONS CONCERNING ITS SERVICE

AMERICAN RED CROSS CLUBMOBILE "SOMEWHERE" IN GREAT BRITAIN

"SIGHTED SINKERS — SANK SAME."

PASSED BY U.S. ARMY CENSOR No. 21 E.T.O., U.S.A.

in the Clubmobile Newsletter, The Sinker (presumably named for their featured donut product), there were three additions, one from St. Louis, one from Kansas City, and Jean Rayl from Springfield. In all, I counted 17 Missourians who served as Clubmobilers during the war, only one from Springfield. It was clearly a select group.

A letter of the same date (July 24th) read in part:

My chances for Clubmobile are very promising at this point. Keep your fingers crossed for me - it seems almost too good to be true.

We have had the pleasure of seeing and hearing the robot bombs – better known over here as the "doodle bug." They're really quite amazing. I guess we'll just have to take it like the English – "Just a bit of a nuisance to have to cope with!" They're really a wonderful people – I admire them even more than I did.

Don't ask a lot of questions – I will write what I can. I only wish you could be here to share all of this excitement and adventure with me... .

And, a letter several days later:

I can safely say I am now in Clubmobile – this of course thrills me to death. I start my training tomorrow. Before we're through we'll know how to operate a doughnut machine, drive the mobile vehicle, make coffee, etc. We have also been issued a "battle-dress" which consists of two pairs of slacks, jacket, fleece-lined boots, wool-lined raincoat and hood, field boots, and wool socks. It's nice looking issue, and very practical." [And then] *"Who should I run into but Ben Parnell! He joined our little tour (of London) and we had a very nice visit... .*

We know by now about Ben Parnell, but what about this "Clubmobile" that my mother was so excited about? What was a Clubmobile, or a Clubmobile Unit, or a Clubmobile Group?

A Clubmobile was a specially outfitted English Bedford truck, readied for combat conditions, driven and staffed by three Red Cross "girls." They used that word so casually, even loosely. Why not women, for indeed, these were women of the bravest order. Girls? The mission of these women was to provide coffee, donuts, cigarettes, music, and good cheer to front line troops, as well as:

"to render our fighting men the greatest possible measure of service on behalf of the American people...and maintain the very highest ideals which inspire the purpose of the American Red Cross." (per Harvey D. Gibson, then Commissioner of the ARC for Great Britain and Europe. This was not child's play.)

Clubmobiles were named: The St. Louis, The Idaho, The Dixie Queen, The President Lincoln (Abe). Mom said that they tended to take on the personality of their "handle" and their handlers.

Organizationally speaking, the Clubmobile Group was the highest order, at least in a local context. The Group consisted of 8 Clubmobiles, 4 supply trucks, 4 Hillman 10 h.p. utility vans, 1 Hillman spare parts van, 8 quarter ton trailers, 2 generator trailers, 1 field range trailer, and 1 water tank trailer. The Group Supervisor was male, each Group Captain female. Thirty young women were assigned to each group, 3 to a Clubmobile, 6 in reserve.

The Clubmobile Unit was one of four in each Group, and included 2 of the Clubmobiles, a supply truck, a utility van, and 2 of the quarter ton trailers. A unit "radiated" from Group HQ and the remaining vehicles and personnel. Curious term, "radiate." Webster says, 1) to branch out in lines from a center, and 2) to spread happiness, love, etc. They no doubt did both.

The Clubmobile Division of the ARC, of which the Clubmobile Group was a part, reported through the Club Service Department, along side the Field Service Department with its Hospital and Home Services Groups. Only one additional organizational layer separated them from Mr. Gibson, pretty flat by military standards.

Technically, Mom was among the ARC personnel assigned to XIX Corp of the U. S. Army. I can only assume that XIX Corp was an umbrella for combat units.

Battlestars & Doughnuts

American Red Cross Clubmobile

"President Lincoln"

World War II Clubmobile Experiences of
Mary Metcalfe Rexford
by
Oscar Whitelaw Rexford

Evidently, Gen. Eisenhower had requested Clubmobile support of invasion forces as early as mid-1943, because of its perceived effectiveness in lifting soldiers' morale.

Ten Clubmobile Groups were assigned to the Continent. Mom served in Clubmobile Group C on the ground in Europe, after training with other Groups in Southern England. Group C's storied history, which included landing on Omaha Beach July 27, 1944, barely 50 days after the blood was spilled, and the subsequent liberation of Paris, is well chronicled in the front pages of Mom's scrapbook. She joined them as they followed our troops into Holland in the fall of '44.

While this organizational meandering is cumbersome, it helped me put her role in perspective. If you want to know more about Clubmobiles, Oscar Rexford has provided an informative look in his book Battlestars and Doughnuts. He recorded the adventures of his wife, and Mom's friend, Chichi Metcalfe, of St. Louis and Clubmobile Group A. He complained in his forward about the lack of references, finding only two books, The ARC in the Storm (Morgan), and At His Side (Korson) on the subject. He wrote to correct the historical slighting of their heroism. But, this is not about history – it is about Mom. History is a bystander, and not a very innocent one, in her story.

FRI – JULY 28
Learned all about the donut machine.

SAT – JULY 29
Same

MON – JULY 31
Learned how to make donuts.

It is obvious that donuts did not move her. But then again, what more to say about donuts?

From a letter, same date, a bit more enthusiasm:

> *I spent my day in a Clubmobile making doughnuts – 10 pounds or 185 of them to be exact. It's really great sport if you don't eat too many.*

Donut making as sport? Keeping score?

CHAPTER 6

#3 Elliott Street

TUES, August 1
Learned that my first assignment in Club-
mobile is to be in Plymouth. I was assigned
to Unit A.

WED, August 2
Today we left for Plymouth. For supper on the
train we opened my K-ration. We ate it in the
lavatory because of the English.

We ate it in the lavatory? Must have been pretty
pukey stuff.

THUR, August 3
Met Nance and Eleanor – my crew. Nance is
Captain. Both wonderful girls.

THUR, August 10
Moved from the hotel to #3 Elliott. It is a 4 room
flat – 2 bedrooms, living room, and kitchen
with bathtub in middle of room. Fortunately,
we eat all of our meals at officer's mess, Ragland
(Barracks).

These few entries framed the next several months
of my mom's life – Plymouth, Nance and Eleanor, #3
Elliott St., and Ragland. Call it the calm before the
storm in her tour of duty.

Mom's communicative efforts shift from diary to letters at this point. Sporadic diary entries carry through
mid-September, then cease altogether. Letters and pictures carry the day thereafter. The words are all hers.

Friday, August 5, 1944
Somewhere in England
Letter #4

Dearest Folks,
*   Sorry I've been so long writing again. My*
time is not my own anymore. I have started on

my new assignment and love it. I'm now quite
a distance from London in a very beautiful
part of England.
*   I thought of you especially Wed., Aug. 2nd.*
It doesn't seem possible that a whole year has
passed since our tragedy. I'm so thankful they
chose that day to send me on my new assign-
ment. I was so busy packing and traveling that
I didn't have much time to think which made it
much easier. The busier I am, the better I like
it – that's why I love this work, there's never a
spare moment to waste.

We're moving into a new flat Wed. – the three of us. It's luxury compared to what we've been having. We have a bedroom (3 beds), kitchen, and sitting room. I had to laugh when we walked in and saw the bathtub in the middle of the kitchen. From now on we'll be doing our bathing in the kitchen. We eat all of our meals out, so it really doesn't matter.

I would love to have film of any size if you can possibly get it. Maybe I can get someone to take pictures for me, they would be priceless to me sometime. I would also love to have some of your divinity, Mother. My mouth waters when I think of it.

Please don't worry, I'm well and happy.

All my love, "Jeannie Bug"

Scrawled on the back of the envelope in my grandfather's hand were the words "Divinity" and "Film." I am guessing she shortly received both.

Mon., Aug. 7, 1944
Somewhere in England
Letter #5

Dearest Folks,

At last your mail has started coming through. I received two nice long letters from you Sat., Mother, and my morale was lifted 100%. You'll never know what your letters mean to me – I can understand now how Johnnie must have felt.

I'm crazy about my new work. I drove our Bedford today for the first time. It was my first experience at driving a truck. It seems so odd to have the steering wheel on the right side, and to drive on the left.

Ironically, Mom would wed Dad two years and one day hence, and birth me eleven months to the day after that. So much death and life between August 1943 and August 1947, personally and universally.

Thursday, August 10, 1944
Somewhere in England
Letter #6

Dearest folks,
I've never appreciated mail so much in my

life. I'm not homesick (except sometimes), but I feel so terrible far away from everything.

We have a weekly schedule to go by. We usually make our doughnuts in the morning and travel in the afternoon. We produce 1,000 doughnuts a day on our little machine – it's lots of fun. Thursday is our day off – it always goes much too fast.

This letter, written August 10, was postmarked "August 11, 1944, U.S. Army Postal Service" on the envelope, and "September 16, 1944, Springfield, Mo., Commercial Sta." on a page of the letter inside. Opened twice before delivery? This is a foreign concept to me.

August 23, 1944
England
Letter #?

Dearest folks,
After receiving five more letters from you

today, I felt so inspired I had to drop you a line. Mother, you can always write such interesting letters. I'm sorry I haven't been able to tell you more about my work or where I am – it must be very annoying to you. So you think I'm in France by now. I only wish I were. I'll probably be sitting here in England when the war is over. I may get to go eventually – after all the excitement is over. I'm afraid I got in too late for any of that "front line stuff" – aren't you relieved!

(Hang on to your pretty little Red Cross hat Mom.)

As I've told you before – Clubmobile is the most wonderful branch of the R.C. It's not easy – I've never worked harder in my life. It's just exactly what I need right now. I arise at seven every morning and have a nice warm breakfast - not coffee and doughnuts! It's usually 8 o'clock before we get started. We oil our machine, mix

our prepared flour, and make our doughnuts. Each batch usually turns out around 300 doughnuts. We average about 3 batches a day. After the "sinkers" are made, the truck has to be cleaned – thoroughly too. We scrub everything in it, including the floor and ourselves – dough is rather messy you know. After lunch, we make our coffee and fill our wares, then we're ready to travel. Some days we go out as far as 35-40 miles. You really know you've been someplace after bumping around in that Bedford all day. We serve from 2 to 4 groups a day, depending on the distance. It's usually 5:30 or 6:00 before we return and have our supper. The truck must be cleaned after serving as well as before, so we spend the early part of the evening doing this. We hardly ever get home before 7:30 in the evening – sometimes as late as 11:00. You can see how little time we have for ourselves.

I'm afraid you have the idea I never get a chance to be a lady anymore. We dress up once in a while and go to a dance or movie. You'll be asking for my autograph when I tell you about my invitation for next Monday night. Lady Astor is giving a ball and I was fortunate

enough to get invited. A Lt. Saddler from Mo. has asked me to go. It's my first date with him but he seems very nice. He went to school in Bolivar. I'm still a bit dubious as to what a Lady expects of her guests – guess I'll soon know. I'll try to remember every little detail Mother, so I can tell you.

I guess you will remember what happened a year ago today. I'll never forget. It's not pleasant to talk about but I can't seem to get it off my mind. That's the reason it's best for me to keep busy. The less time I have to think, the *better off I am. I just want to tell you again how much I appreciate the wonderful way you both have accepted all of this. You've been wonderful parents.*

This line I started out to write has turned out to be an epistle. This is really the first chance I've had to sit down and collect my thoughts since I've been here. I hope I haven't worn you out with all this chatter, but I had to take it out on someone. All my love to you both. "Jeannie Bug"

(More on Lady Astor from her next letter, #11, August 31st)

I attended Lady Astor's Ball last Mon. night. She seems to be quite busy these days and couldn't be there. The old Lord himself filled in for her. He's a very charming old gent and much more popular than she. It was a typical "limey" dance – pretty much of a flop as far as the Americans were concerned, but the English had a wonderful time. Glenn Miller and his famous Army band happened to be here in person that same night. The party broke up early and we all progressed to the theatre to hear him. It was wonderful – the best band I've ever had the pleasure of listening to. It really is something to attend a Lady Astor party and Glenn Miller all in the same evening. Most everyone had on "civies" except the military and the Red Cross. I wore my summer dress uniform.

Same letter, more mundane matters.

I am enclosing some heather I picked today – especially for you mother. I'm afraid it won't be much by the time it reaches the states. I only wish you could see it growing – the fields are the most beautiful shade of lavender.

Eleanor brought my footlocker with her from London, otherwise, I wouldn't have it yet. It was almost like receiving a Christmas box it's been so long since I packed it – 55 days. It's quite amusing to look over the useless things I brought – just excess luggage as far as

10203 AT PORTHGWARRA CORNWALL – JUDGES LTD

I'm concerned.

I'm always in such a rush – every minute counts. I'm going to spend my old age just taking it easy and most of all, not rushing – ha! ha!. I love you both more than anything in the world...

To set matters straight, Mom may have lost a step or two, but is still rushing more than most at age 83.

I must admit to wrestling with perspective as I share the weekly, if not daily, history of these perilous times through the eyes of my young mother. So, please forgive

TORQUAY, VANE HILL · 75738

me if I go back and forth in time to gain it. In this instance it is the date September, 1. Mom had no letters "to" or "from" on that date. Yet the importance of "September 1st" in the life of mankind and my mother is striking. Germany invaded Poland on September 1, 1939, to begin World War II. Five years later to the day, Mom was in Europe to avenge the death of her husband through acts of kindness and service for men seeking to stop the Nazi death machine and save the world for me and mine to follow.

These acts were of a personal but wholesome nature somewhat at odds with the stereotypical independent woman of the new millennium. They did not speak to female liberation or freedom – professional, intellectual, or sexual. At the same time it is that word "independent" that to me defines Mom's journey through grief to reconciliation of her loss with a new future. I find innocence, maturity, wonder, sadness, naivety, anger, and energy in her words, and bravery in her rush to self-reclamation in this specific crucible of space and time.

September 4, 1944
Letter #12

You'll never know how it hurt me to hear about the Reed men. I'm awfully glad you told me though. Poor Mrs. Reed. The shock must have been almost unbearable. Somehow I always felt that little Ollie would get through this thing. I didn't even know Col. Reed was able to go overseas – he was quite ill from malaria.

This was apparently a father/son war loss. I recall visiting a family in Branson as a boy. They lived deep in the woods, and my parents would take us to their place after church on occasion. They lost their only two sons to WWII on the same day. They were outwardly strong, but even my immature senses registered their anger and cynicism. I simply can't imagine what they must have buried deep within themselves when they buried their sons.

You've probably guessed by now that we're attached to an outfit. We were quite pleased and "set up" to learn that the commanding officer had sent in a letter of commendation to our headquarters about the "St. Louis" and its crew. The letter read as follows:

1) (a) It has come to my attention that the Red Cross Clubmobile is rendering exceedingly valuable service to the troops attached and assigned to this Headquarters.

(b) For example, on [date deleted], 1944, the Clubmobile captained by Nance Krone, assisted by Eleanor Campbell and Jean Rayl, began serving doughnuts and coffee at 0600 hours, continued throughout the day until late at night during the troop movement, a period of approximately 18 hours of sustained effort.

(c) This fine work was of great value in maintaining high morale among the troops.

2) In view of the forgoing, it is requested that you convey my official appreciation, thanks, and commendation to the above listed ladies of the American Red Cross.

This of course is not for publication, but it does make you feel better to know that you are doing the boys some good. I couldn't send the letter or fill in the date because of names and locations.

P.S. The war news is certainly encouraging. I knew "old Patton" would come to the rescue.

No sooner was the "St. Louis" commended than ditched for a larger version, with an extra crew member.

Saturday, Sept. 8, 1944
Letter #13

We received a new Clubmobile Thursday to replace the "St. Louis." I'm now a member of the "Idaho." This is a much better truck in spite of the name.

We serve coffee with our doughnuts because we don't want the boys to choke to death! We also hand out candy, cigarettes, and post cards

– all for free too. We're not allowed to serve the English soldiers – I'll explain it to you sometime.

I'm enclosing a couple of pictures taken recently – "sad sack" Rayl they call me.

Another date pops out – not the Sept. 8 of the letter, but the September 11 of the postmark, imposed on the 6 cent stamp of an American bomber, 57 years before the day that would likely define my generation's space and time. For some reason Mom's diary takes over her story for the next several weeks, then stops forever. Not sure why, perhaps it was the travel.

TUES – SEPT 12
Lt. Larry Saddler and I walked over to St. Andrews Church to hear the bells. This church was built in 1460, and blitzed on March 20 and 21, 1941. Walls are 12 feet thick. It's the 3rd oldest church in England, having survived the attack almost 500 years later. Also went to Stonehenge. Its rocks date back to 2500 BC. Altars hand-carved, some still standing in upright position. Individual rocks weigh many tons, and were probably dragged hundreds of miles by ancient unknown people. The horizontal altar fastened in place on two upright stones by hand-carved tongue and groove.

I recall visiting Stonehenge as a college student on a cold rainy day, no one else around, and being absolutely spooked. It resonated with melancholy and shadowy visages. That was 24 years after Mom was there. That it has survived the ravages of time, war, and tourists leads to a deeper thought, but I'm not sure I want to venture there. It is simply the strangest place I have ever visited. Mom's perspective is substantially sounder.

THURS – SEPT 14
Served troops at Fowey. A Major took us out in his little motor boat. We went up and down the Fowey River. We saw the home of Daphne De-Mauier, a very quaint little green house overlooking the water. Further down, we saw two huge Liberty Ships docked.

SOMEWHERE ON THE ENGLISH COAST — A Harbour Craft Battalion helps the American Red
Cross Clubmobile Girls load up coffee and doughnuts for their next assignment.

Left to right: Nance Krone (Captain) daughter of Mr. and Mrs. C.F. Krone, 7 Bridges,
Chappaqua, N.Y.; Cpl. Edward G. Freitas, 1332 S. Rampart, New Orleans, whose wife
Mrs. E.G. Freitas lives at that address; Pfc. Robey A. Johnson, whose wife Mrs.
Marylin Johnson lives at 4412 Allison St., Norwood, Ohio; Miss Eleanor Campbell,
Kenwood Apartments, Great Neck, Long Island; Mrs. Jean Reyl, daughter of Mr. and
Mrs. J. Wyman Hogg, 1125 Benton Avenue, Springfield, Mo. and (in tin hat) Cpl.
Henry Costello, whose wife Mrs. Jo Costello lives at 497 Breckenridge, Buffalo,
N.Y.

B 1923

Photo by: Ronald Ockenden
             Red Cross Correspondent

Greene

SAT – SEPT 16
We had a steak feed in our flat with steaks from the Navy. I received a wire telling me to report to London for ranging and spent the rest of the night packing.

SUN – SEPT 17
Took a sleeper out of London Sun. night with three girls for Greenock (Scot.).

MON – SEPT 18
Arrived in Glasgow 6:45 this morning. Caught the 7:00 train for Greenock. Arrived around 8:00.

TUES – SEPT 19
Worked at Princess Docks nine hours today, meeting troops from Isle de France. Most of them are replacements and will go right into combat – Information and Air Corps.

WED – SEPT 20
Worked at the docks again. When we arrived back in Greenock, learned our ranging was over.

Mom's diary ends with a sentence beginning with "Leadpipe…" – doubt that I will ever know where that was headed. Letters resume upon her return to quarters.

Saturday, September 23, 1944
Somewhere in England

I received my ballot today, which means I can vote. Nance and Eleanor are really 'griped' because they both come from NY and can't. It's just as well though because they're both for Dewey. I never dreamed I would cast my first ballot from foreign shores. I feel very fortunate to get the opportunity.

She did not number this letter. It was brief, but did contain a political observation that serves as a reminder as to one reason we were fighting this war. Read this children, and never forget to vote.

Mom's next letter was dated Sept. 27, and was noteworthy for only one reason – the postmark inside was "Springfield, Mo., Nov. 15" – almost two months

42

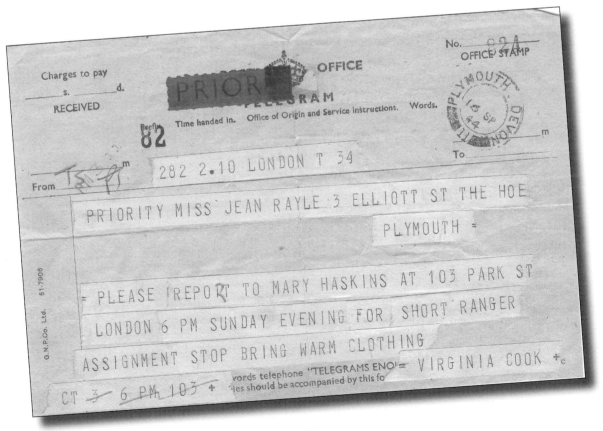

to delivery. I can't imagine as a parent waiting two months to hear from my daughter at war, let alone not knowing that at time of receipt of this innocuous letter, #18, she was heading to the front lines, far from the relative safety of southwest England. Better not to know I guess.

One letter in the box from this time frame moved me. It was from a Pvt. Cecil P. Simpson and carried the date 9/15. Private Simpson had obviously been touched by Mom's kindness somewhere along the doughnut line, and expressed his appreciation in sincere, if marginally literate, terms.

hello my Dear Frind,
    as I have Just left you I thought I would try to write to you to Show you at I do like you and hope you will say the same about me. well pal, I hope this letter well find you well and enjoy life. well pal, I am going to church to night and you no I will rumber you in my pary and hope you well rumber me in your pary. well pal, I am going to stop my Drinking and see if I can't be a better boy. well pal, if I don't get to see you,

you be good. From Frind Cecil P Simpson to my pal Jeany. God belse you and be with you where every you go. good night pal.

Wonder if Mom wrote Cecil back. Wonder if Cecil made it.

Mom's scrapbook carries faded pictures of troops at Fowey, "Sea-Bees" at Sandridge, troops at Chattleswood and Oakhampton, troops of G-75 in Plymouth, all under the notation "Served these troops from Aug-Oct, 1944." Most of the soldiers wore smiles, some posed with the ladies, some in larger groups, some named, some not.

October 1, 1944
Letter # 19

Dearest Mother,
    Since tomorrow is your birthday, I thought I would write this especially to you. Of course it will be late getting there, but at least you'll know you are especially in my thoughts.
    I couldn't help remembering another birth-

44

day, September 29th – he would have been 24.
Guess this makes you wonder if I'm homesick
or unhappy. I can honestly state that I'm not
in the least. Of course, I miss you and Daddy
more than anything in the world, but I'm sure
it won't be long before this awful war is over
and we're all together again. I can't thank you
all enough for being so wonderful about letting
me come. You've certainly been unselfish about
the whole thing.

October 4, 1944
Letter #20

Dearest Mother,
    I was quite amused at your sleuthing "Mrs.

Ellery Queen Hogg." I'm afraid you'll never learn
my whereabouts if you try to trace me through
Lady Astor – she lives all over England! It was
a good try anyway.
    I still love my work as much as ever. You can't
imagine how inspiring it can be. I only wish
I could tell you more about it – I'm afraid I'll
forget before I get home.
    I washed my hair tonight and have been
drying it by the fire while writing this. Please
excuse if it doesn't make sense. You can imagine
the confusion I live around.

    The next letter was to my grandfather, and bore the
note "to Daddy about Christmas" in his handwriting
on the envelope. It was only then that I noticed most

letters carried a summary comment from him on the envelope – organizational I suppose. This one indeed focused on his selecting a special Christmas present for my grandmother. "Spend at least $25," Mom instructed. Unlike the others, it was not numbered – extra top secret I guess.

October 10, 1944 (postmark inside indicated

January 28, 1945 receipt, almost 4 months)
Letter #21

Dearest Mother,
We've really put in a day and I'm a little "pooped." We broke the record in donut production today by turning out 12 batches (or 3,600). At this point I even feel like a donut.

No wonder I can't even eat one any more.

I was quite interested in your gossip about Captain Packard and Margaret. I wasn't surprised about Packard, but was terribly shocked about Margaret. Do you suppose it is really true?

So much for the innocence I keep sensing.

October 14, 1944
Letter #22
Somewhere in England

Dearest Mother,
Well, at last my wish has been granted....

Mom was being forwarded to London for deployment, though she would/could say nothing more than those words above. More entertaining were her observations about my father to be. His good friends had stopped to see my Grandmother Hogg, who had evidently reported immediately to Mom.

I was quite amused over your comments on Ben. I didn't know he'd ever gotten serious over any girl—he has certainly made the rounds. I'm sorry he was "jilted"—he is a very nice person. I'm afraid Ben's and my attraction for each other is mutual—friendship basis only.

Friends and spouses for 56 years and counting!

The next round of letters, numbers 23 through 31, were sent from London, and carry a hint of frustration tucked between layers of awe.

October 21, 1944—I'm now in London the past few days with Nance and Eleanor. We're going on our new assignment together as a crew which thrills us to death.

October 23, 1944—I can't get over this civilized life I've been leading the past few days here in London. I hardly know how to act. It won't last for long so we might as well enjoy it. You don't know how we're enjoying being ladies

once again – I'm afraid we're going to get "soft" again though.

October 27, 1944 – We're still sitting around London awaiting assignment – getting softer by the minute. We're not liking it a bit!

October 31, 1944 – Well, here I am still in London awaiting that new assignment I've been talking about so long. I'm rather disgusted at this point. I hate being idle for such a long period of time after having been so busy and thoroughly absorbed in my work the past 3 months.

November 3, 1944 – It doesn't seem possible that 5 whole months have passed since I left home – in some ways though it seems like years. I know these last few letters must seem terrible dull, but there just isn't anything I can tell you.

Dispersed within are references to a likely distant relative: "a Scottish girl I met from the Douglas clan, mother's maiden name Hogg," and the election: "maybe my little vote will do some good," and "I'm so proud that I was able to have a part in this election…I pray that the war will be over before we go through this

again." Oh yes, there was the cursory "Ben" reference, this one on 10/31: "I've tried several times to contact Ben since I've been in London. They haven't given me much satisfaction at his headquarters – I just know that he's out of town at the present time. Oh well, I tried…."

And then the letter she had been waiting to write.

Saturday, November 18, 1944
Letter #32
Dearest folks,
*   Well here I am – this time in Paris!*

She was on her way to the front lines.

CHAPTER 7

Hammered in Heerlen

Mom didn't stay long in Paris, and I sensed from the few letters that her mind was already somewhere beyond.

More from the November 18 letter:

> *I'm to be sent to Holland in the near future. I'm so thrilled over this – guess I've just been living right. The only disappointing part is that I have to be separated from Nance and Eleanor – they're to be stationed in France together. Guess I'll have to close for now. The lights have all gone out and this candle I'm trying to write by is about to put out my eyes. This is war you know, so you can expect anything. Things are going to be different from now on.*

November 21, 1944
Paris
Letter #34

Dearest Folks,
  Guess this will be the last chance to write for a few days. I'm leaving tomorrow on my

new assignment. I can't tell you how excited I am about going.
  Right now I'm sitting in a downstairs beauty salon having my hair set. I thought I would be a lady just once more. Besides, we're allowed two baths a week here, so I can imagine what it will be like where I'm going. There isn't such a thing as heat in Paris, and you know how cold it can be in November.
  I'm so thankful for this work – especially at

26.11.44

50

certain times. I can't help remembering three years ago today. I'm so absorbed though, it makes everything seem easier.

Mom had married her childhood sweetheart three years ago to the day, November 21, 1941, a lifetime away.

November 24, 1944
Letter #35

Dearest Folks,
Hope you had a very pleasant Thanksgiving – you were in my thoughts more than ever yesterday. I had a very pleasant day in spite of the fact I spent most of it in the back of a GMC truck. We had our dinner at an "M.P." camp in Belgium. It's the best meal I've had since I left the states.
I can't begin to tell you all of the interesting things I've seen and done the past few days. The sight of Aachen is something I will never forget.

You just can't visualize how badly that city is torn up. It seems horrible that such a hideous thing as war has to exist among civilized people – I pray to God this will be the last one.
I can't tell you how happy I am in my new assignment. Each one gets better and more exciting. We have a wonderful set-up here. We're living in a hotel (The Neerlandia) with heat and hot and cold running water – something unheard of over here. I had my first bath in six days today.

Two days later, November 26, 1944, the "wonderful set-up," the "hotel with heat and hot and cold running water" was gone, bombed into abandonment by a German 280mm railway propelled gun. These guns were moved in and out of railroad tunnels to escape allied bombing runs. They fired on Heerlen several nights in a row, first destroying buildings around The Neerlandia, killing several civilians, spraying shrapnel through hotel rooms, finally zeroing in on the hotel itself. Mom and 30 of her comrades were meeting in

Mom's room
at the Hotel
Neerlandia on
November, 28
1944

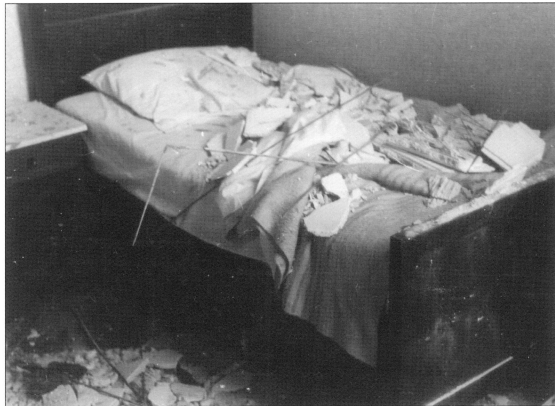

the hotel dining room about 10:30 p.m., listening as the explosions grew louder and closer. Finally a dead hit on the kitchen sent Mom diving under a table. The ladies scrambled to the basement, only to retreat outside because of escaping gas.

They spent a shaky night at the Officer's Club before transferring to a maternity hospital. The hotel was uninhabitable. They had dodged a big bullet. From Mom's scrapbook clippings I read comments from an observer to

the destruction: "The girls, without exception, were grand. It was a trying experience but there was no complaining, no confusion, no hysteria, no evidence of fear, they laughed, joked and kidded each other …. Watching these American girls we felt a surge of pride.

Pride in belonging to a country blessed with such women. Pride in their spirit, their willingness to risk whatever comes in order to do their bit to help win the war ….They take doughnuts and coffee as far forward as commanders will allow."

53

November 28, 1944
Letter #36
Dearest Folks,

Hope you'll forgive me if you don't hear from me as often as you have been — I'll be busier from now on. My work is even more exciting than it was back in Plymouth. I only wish I could tell you more about it, but I'm even more restricted than I was, if you know what I mean. Maybe I won't forget too much before I get back.

She seemed very calm, and I'm quite certain that her parents gratefully did not learn of the shelling of The Hotel Neerlandia until she returned home.

December 3, 1944
Letter #37

Dearest Folks,

My work varies each day — sometimes I cook, but most of the time I serve. Last Sunday six of us made over 13,000 doughnuts so you can see we're not loafing. The boys are much bigger "chow hounds" up here than they were in England. I'm still crazy about my new work — it's more "rugged" but much more exciting.

December 8, 1944
Letter#38
(somewhere in Holland)

Dearest Folks,
December 6 was the Dutch "Sint Nicholaas"

day. Everyone in this country exchanges gifts that day — December 25th is set aside for worship only. You can't imagine the fun we had at the Red Cross club here in town helping the children celebrate this occasion. They even arranged to have "Sint Nicholaas," attired in a purple robe and crown, with a staff, and his aide Peter. The children are made to believe he comes from Spain bearing their gifts (instead of the north pole). Peter comes along to take all of the bad children back to Spain. Each child lives in constant fear of this happening to him or her. The club was full of "GI's" and I think they got a bigger kick out of it than the children.

December 11, 1944
Letter #39

Dearest Folks,

I had a letter from Eleanor Campbell yesterday informing me that Ben is in Paris. I fortunately failed to check out of the hotel when I left and he was able to make connections through them. I, of course, can't see him until I go in, and that won't be until I get a leave. We're supposed to get seven days every four months, but unfortunately I was en-route when mine came due. Maybe I can work something out yet. Fate has certainly brought us together in some odd places hasn't it? If I had only known the four days I was there, I could have at least seen him.

December 16, 1944
Letter #40
Somewhere in Holland

Dearest Folks,

Yesterday was certainly a "red letter day" for me. I received my first mail since Paris – over 20 letters. I feel very fortunate to have received anything – my APO has been changed so many times.

There's one thing I want to mention in this letter before closing and that's about Annabelle. I'm going to make a suggestion and if you approve start acting immediately. I'm so glad she's at last doing something about her condition. I'm afraid she will get discouraged before the treatment is over because of the expense. I know how "hard hit" she probably is at this time and would like to help out. Do you think she would be offended at such a suggestion? There wouldn't be any obligation or interest to pay – it wouldn't matter if she were never able to pay it back. It would be a wonderful investment on my part just to see her free from this affliction. Please don't think I am bragging or over-confident just because I have a few dollars stashed away. Money ceases to be of any value to you when you can't enjoy spending it, and this is my idea of a good way to start. This is just between us if you think it advisable.

Don't know Annabelle or what her "condition" was, but I was touched by Mom's gesture. She has always been a giver.

> *I pray to God that this horrible thing will be over this time next year and we can all celebrate (Christmas) together.*

Mom's wish was to come true, but not before things got worse before better. On the day Mom wrote this letter Hitler launched a counter-offensive igniting the Battle of the Bulge. The following day 140 Americans were taken prisoner, and 86 were shot on the road to Malmedy. I unfolded Mom's table sized map of western Europe with many of her points of visitation circled in pen. I was able to locate Malmedy and estimate that Aachen, Germany, Clubmobile Group C's post during most of the battle was less than fifty miles away from the slaughter.

CHAPTER 8

New Year's at the Bulge

The Battle of the Bulge (so named because Hitler's desperate attempt to split Allied forces and retake the vital seaport of Antwerp produced only a "bulge" in the good guy's line of control) began on December 16, 1944, and lasted through most of January. It was our troops' largest land battle of the war, and involved more than a million soldiers, nearly half of whom were American. 19,000 Americans lost their lives, 60,000 were wounded or captured. Books have been written about the battle, Hitler's gamble for "the big solution" in the face of the Russian advance from the east, intense American bombing of the homeland, a recent assassination attempt, and the bitter conditions under which the battle was waged. The allies prevailed, and the end of the war took form. But then this is about Mom.

December 21, 1944
Letter #41

Dearest Folks,

I'm really beginning to get the Christmas spirit now. Every clubmobile has a beautifully decorated tree and Christmas records to make it complete – the boys love it! I am permanently assigned to a clubmobile – the "Dixie Queen." Up until now I have been serving from first one and then another. It's much better to be permanently assigned. I'd give anything if I could tell you more about my work, but that will just have to wait.

I haven't told you much about my travels since I've been over here, for security reasons. Counting England, I touched six countries in a week's time – that's really traveling isn't it? I have been in Germany several times which you've probably already guessed by now.

I'm not homesick, but relish the thought of this horrible war ending someday so we can come back home to our normal peaceful lives

in "good old" Springfield. You'll probably have to train me all over again just like you would train "Chappie" [family dog], and I don't mean what you're thinking! It just that I have listened to "GI" lingo and slang for so many months I won't be able to understand good old hillbilly talk.

I have been much busier than usual – you can probably guess why.

This last line is her only reference to what the whole world knew was going on in the Ardennes, and to the significance of the subsequent thirty days to the outcome of the war. Sadly, just one day before that letter was dated, Katie (Ann Kathleen) Cullen became the first American Red Cross girl to die through enemy action on the Western front. On the morning that she was to return to Clubmobile Group B in Herve, Belgium from a field hospital she was killed in a bomb strike. She was buried in an American Cemetery at Henri la Chapelle. For some reason Mom's "dog tag" slipped into the back of mind as I read about Katie and stared into the serious young face that flanked her story. I went back to the scrapbook and massaged the stamped metal piece once again. ARC 43666 T44B. It felt cold.

Mom tells a story about being convinced she was going to die during this period in Aachen. One evening, she took a bottle of wine from the hotel bar and returned to her room after dinner. She recalls "drinking it all, to the very last drop." She awoke alive, but not well! This fear does not show in her letters.

December 26, 1944
Letter #43

Dearest Folks,

You will be pleased to know that I had the nicest Christmas I could have possibly had away from you all. Christmas morning we all gathered

around our big tree at the hotel and handed out a silly gift to the person whose name we had drawn. We had breakfast before going out to serve – fresh eggs and everything. We then left for Germany to serve the particular outfit of our choice. Instead of doughnuts this time we passed out Christmas packages. Some contained lovely Red Cross sweaters, and others candy, cigars, pipe tobacco, scarves, chewing gum, and utility kits. It was quite a thrill to see their reaction to this attention – they were like little boys with new toys. I guess we never will know just how much they really did appreciate it.

I enjoyed Christmas dinner until I got to thinking about those poor boys upon the front lines eating "C and K" rations while we non-combatants sat back enjoying life. War is such a horrible thing – I pray to God I never live to see another. It is utterly useless – I realize it even more after living around it. I can understand now why the boys never want to discuss it when they are around – it's something you want to forget and fast!

Mom never did forget, and when Viet Nam ripped apart our nation and riled our family, she calmed the latter and soothed macho rhetoric at both ends of our spectrum with the credibility of one who had served and the genuine remorse of one who hoped to "never live to see another." Like most mothers she did not want her sons fighting there, but it was deeper than that. I know now, after reading this letter for the first time that it also related to the horror of her first-hand experience with war, and her wish for human kind to rise above it.

Maybe we can all celebrate the next Christmas together. All my love to the most wonderful parents in the whole world, "Jeannie Bug"

It was on this day that General Patton broke through to relieve the siege of Bastogne, effectively stopping the German advance.

December 29, 1944
Letter #44
Somewhere in Germany

Dearest Mother,
You can see from my letterhead that we are now living in Germany. We are living in a hotel that has heat, water and electricity. I don't know what we've done to deserve all of this. We, of course, can't fraternize with the German people.

January 2, 1945
Letter #45
Somewhere in Germany

Dearest Folks,
This is the first letter I have attempted to write in 1945 – I have so little time anymore. Saturday, as you know, was my birthday and I wasn't allowed to forget it for a minute. Lou, our Red Cross mess sergeant, presented me with a lovely cake and we had quite a celebration. My prize gift of the day was a fresh egg from Belgium given to me by one of the girls in the group. This may sound silly but those things are all as scarce as gasoline at home.

Yesterday we served an engineer outfit and who should be the commanding officer but Maj. Bob Tabb of Lexington, Mo. He knew Johnnie very well. He remembered him at Wentworth and West Point and we had so much fun reminiscing. He couldn't seem to say enough about Johnnie and how well thought of he was. You don't know how good this made me feel.

I'm taking my seven-day leave next week with two other girls from the group. We're spending most of it in Paris. Hope "good old Ben" is still there so he can show me around. I was due this leave two months ago but don't feel right even taking it now – there's so much to be done up here.

You asked in your letter how long I would

be over here – I frankly don't know. I'll probably be lucky if I'm home this time next year – don't count on it too much. I'm praying that this whole mad affair will be over shortly and we'll all be home, but you never know.

On January 8, 1945, Hitler ordered his troops to begin a retreat from the tip of the "Bulge." He was fearful of being squeezed by Patton from the south and Montgomery from the west. It took only five more days for American and British forces to join up and retake the "Bulge," and only a few more after that to restore the original front line. Shortly thereafter Mom began her leave.

January 11, 1945
Letter #46
Paris

Dearest Folks,
*   We arrived in Paris after a very hard trip in*

our Red Cross (English Hillman) truck. It's a very breezy vehicle and we had horrible weather all of the way. The Red Cross put us up in a nice hotel with hot baths and soft beds. We spent one night in Brussels (on the way).

*   I received a nice letter from Ben just before leaving asking me to contact him if I ever got down this way again. I did that very thing yesterday afternoon. He took me to dinner last night, and then to a party his C.O. was having. They had lots of fun kidding me about being the only person there really fighting this war.*

*   Ben is planning to show me the city during my short stay and I'm certainly looking forward to that. Can you visualize two Missouri hillbillies in Paris?*

January 18, 1945
Letter #47
Somewhere in Germany

Dearest Folks,

Sorry I've been so long writing this time, but it will take me a week to get caught up. Ben was responsible for my trip being such a pleasant one – he was grand to me. It's amazing how much he has changed and you know what I mean! I didn't have a bit of trouble – maybe I've lost my "S.A.," if I ever had any! Just wanted you to know that I am well and safe, and thinking of you all.

January 20, 1945
Letter #48
Germany
Dearest Folks,

Mother, don't ever apologize for writing about every day things – that's what I live to hear. Your letters are such an inspiration to me.

You seem to be worried about my reaction toward you all when I get back home – I have

been worrying about the reverse. I didn't realize until I went to Paris last week just how much I have changed. I feel so "out of place" in a skirt and around civilized human beings anymore. I have lived in slacks and listened to "G.I. lingo" for so long I sometimes wonder what I will be like. I hope you understand that I'm not complaining – it's just that it worries me when I give it much thought.

I was quite interested in your reaction to the counter-attack. Conditions weren't too encouraging over here for a while, but things are beginning to look much brighter again. I admire and respect every boy over here – they have done a beautiful job. They deserve more credit than they will ever get. After seeing the way they live and the hardships they have endured, I thank God that Johnnie was spared them. I am convinced now that there are worse things than death, and this is one of them. We must do a thorough job this time so it will never happen again. This all probably sounds very

morbid and I shouldn't even try to write about it, but sometimes I can't help myself.

I will change the subject back to my trip to Paris. Having been there since mid-Sept., Ben pretty well knows the town. I was entertained very royally and without anything expected in return (if you know what I mean).

I have never seen such beautiful clothes. The prices range on blouses and sweaters from $28-$40, and dresses from $100-$120, so I naturally wasn't in the market for clothes. It doesn't cost to look!

January 23, 1945
Letter #49
Germany

Dearest Folks,
You're probably wondering why this sudden lapse in my correspondence. I have never been so busy in my life and have been appointed assistant mess sgt. to make things more complicated. If

you don't think it isn't a job to plan meals for 35-40 people just try it! All we have to work with are army rations (mostly canned dehydrated foods) and German cooks. You should see us using the "sign language." Besides that I work all day on the clubmobile.

January 27, 1944
Letter #50
Germany

Dearest Folks,

Just about the time you figure out my location I move again. You probably know where I am now – do you remember the town I mentioned going through some time back? We'll probably be here for a while – I hope.

You asked about the boys and their reactions to us. They're simply wonderful – treat us all like queens. I'm afraid we're going to be a spoiled bunch of women when we get home. Some of their favorite remarks are – "Is she really an American woman?" "What are you doing up here?" "Do you really drive that truck?" "Don't put any sugar in mine, just stir it with your finger!" They always ask how long you've been over and what state you're from. When I say Missouri, they usually come back with "Is that in the United States?" I always try to look mad, but without much success. I always wear my wedding ring and sometimes wonder if I should when serving. Somebody always embarrasses himself by asking where my old man is, or making some crack about my already being taken. It doesn't bother me anymore. It's happened so many times, but it's terribly embarrassing for them. I always try to change the subject without answering. I'm crazy about the average "G.I" and my admiration for them never ceases. America has something to be very proud of in their men – they're doing a wonderful job. You just can't realize what they have gone through until you see it – some of them are very pitiful. I could go on for hours about this but won't. There are so many things I want to forget, but I will always remember

Marlena Dietrich
among ruins of
Aachen on New Year's
day 1944

Siegfried Line
Rotgen, Germany
December, 1944

the courage and determination of the American soldier.

We drive our own trucks just like we did back in England. I had never even seen a "G.M.C." Clubmobile until I joined the group back in November. They are quite different from the English Bedford – much heavier (2 1/2 ton) and not nearly so dangerous. They're really a picnic to drive!

And drive Mom did, from base Aachen to serving corps artillery units entrenched in makeshift dugouts in the Hurtgen Forest, to ghost towns like Eschweiler and Ruhe, to Stolberg. Mom's scrapbook read that Aachen was a city of ruins and that despite the cold, most were grateful for the snows, which "softened the scars of Charlemagne's capital." On January 28, 1945, the Battle of the Bulge was officially over. Today, Mom remembers little beyond the brave soldiers she served – faceless, nameless – and her frostbitten hands.

CHAPTER 9

Crossing the Rhine

Mom spent the months after Aachen, trailing and serving American troops as they punched into the heart of "the Homeland." Her scrapbook records stops in Kohlschied, Korschenbroich, Jülich, Neuss, München-Gladbach (home of Herr Goebbels), Düsseldorf, tracking north to Wesel and the crossing of the Rhine, then straight toward Berlin, which she never reached. Some of these towns make her map, some do not or are spelled differently. The common theme throughout this phase of the war were rivers, and the crossing thereof. Everything seemed to focus on reaching a river and finding a means to reach the other side – the Ruhr, the Rhine, the Weser – rivers as objectives, impediments; triumphs over rivers not Germans. Not that simple I'm sure, but the Nazis were on the run at this point, buying time for their scientists to let the atomic genie out of the bottle and turn the tide.

February 2, 1945
Letter #51
Germany

Dearest Folks,
The days are getting longer and so is our work, which gives me even less time (to write). We saw grass today for the first time in six weeks. This is the worst spell of weather most of us have ever experienced. My heart aches for those poor boys living in it – they certainly have courage and determination.

February 3, 1945
Letter #52
Germany

Dearest Folks,
Your reputation as a candy maker broadens with every batch you send – Mrs. Hogg, you're famous! It's a wonder I can get into my uniform

anymore!
I got a bang out of Walt's letters (sister Mary's husband). He's so clever and cute – no wonder Mary loves him so much. If I could find a man like that I might consider getting married again, but there's only one Walt. Speaking of marriage – don't worry your heads about Ben. He isn't interested and neither am I. The more I see of men, the more disgusted I become – I wouldn't trust any of them as far as I can see, and that "ain't far"! I don't know what got me started on this dissertation about men, but let's change the subject!

February 9, 1945
Letter # -
Still somewhere in Germany

Dearest Folks,

I live in such a state of confusion I can't remember what I have written from one time to the next.

Our new home is not quite so "luxurious" as our last. We have neither heat nor water. The army is kind enough to let us use their showers, which is really a lifesaver at this point. If we can just get some heat, we'll be set. When summer and warm weather come we will at least have one less worry. When we sleep out in the field, it's either tents or nothing! I'm not complaining for I realize how much worse off we could be. You certainly learn to appreciate the little things you always took for granted before. It's really the best thing that ever happened to me and I feel very fortunate to be a part of it.

I am terribly intrigued with Daddy's new dress shop. That could be a nice project for me when I get back. Mother, would you go to market with me to help get me started? Oh well,

I have plenty of time to decide my future. The important thing now is to get this war over with and then worry about what's to come.

You're right Mother, it's much better that the folks back home don't and can't realize the awfulness of war. You sometimes wonder if life is worth living when you see the suffering and misery we humans have brought about. I certainly hope the states haven't changed, for these boys are going to need a drastic change when they get back to bring them out of it. That song, "Keep the Home Fires Burning" really means something now. I am one of millions that wants to find my family just as I left them.

I believe Mom was operating out of Kohlschied at this time. I base that on her scrapbook more than anything.

February 12, 1945
Letter #55
Germany

Dearest Folks,
We haven't been able to serve the past few days,

due to the temperamental generators and our recent move. This extra time has been a lifesaver for the "mess sgts." We have spent practically every minute of it in the kitchen training new help and re-arranging our "stores."

Yesterday was our own Col. Goodwin's birthday and we celebrated the occasion last night with a buffet dinner. Lou and I spent the whole day in the kitchen helping the Germans prepare it.

Germans? Germans as in "the enemy"? Preparing the Colonel's food? So who took the first bite? Hopefully that wasn't one of Mom's duties!

I'm afraid I didn't make much of a hit with "good old Ben." I wrote my "bread and butter letter" shortly after my return and have never received an answer. Not that it matters to me.

Maybe I have B.O. or bad breath – I haven't had my teeth cleaned for a long time. Oh me, such is life.

Wonder what a "bread and butter letter" is? Wonder who my Dad to be was celebrating his 26th birthday with in Paris on the very day this was written?

For some reason my grandfather wrote "Private" in bold letters on the outside of this one. Wonder what that was all about? Surely B.O. and bad breath don't warrant double censorship. Much to wonder about here.

February 15, 1945
Letter #56
Somewhere in Germany

Dearest Folks,
Thank you Daddy for that sweet valentine! It arrived on the 13th. I was so touched I

69

Serving 2nd Armored Division at the front.

almost shed tears. How can I ever thank you both for your thoughtfulness – you're wonderful to me.

It was on the day the Valentine arrived that we bombed the German city of Dresden, aka "Florence of the Elbe," due east longitudinally of Mom's position near the Ruhr River and Jülich. In terms of flat out destruction, the fire bombing of Dresden exceeded any effort to date, and to some, any effort since, including Hiroshima, Nagasaki, and Hanoi, Christmas, 1972. Kurt Vonnegut wrote of surviving that night as a prisoner of war in a slaughterhouse. His acerbic, schizophrenic Slaughterhouse Five, published in 1969, should be required reading for anyone enamored of war. I'm thankful Mom wasn't there.

February 22, 1945
Letter # 58

Dearest Folks,
This has been a "virgin" day for me. I had my first bottle of American beer since leaving the states and saw my first "dog-fight." Our air corps knocked down two Jerry planes and I had a grandstand seat for the performance. It's the most enjoyable sight in the world as long as it isn't one of ours going down.

I had my first ride in a tank the other day. Bobbie and I boarded the tank and when asked where we wanted to go replied "give us the works!" He did; we went through fields, over fences and trees, etc. We were slightly shaken up, but none the worse for our experience. We both looked like we had a bad case of freckles from the mud. Didn't have time to wash it off before serving, and the boys got quite a kick out of it.

Our General was in for dinner last night. You won't believe me when I tell you I spent the evening holding hands with him – Betty Grass and me. He's from my part of the country and lots of fun. He's a good rebel and a staunch Democrat so you can imagine what a "good egg" he is. You don't even think about his rank until those stars loom up. If all generals are

like that, they're good enough for my money. We spent most of the evening discussing good food – principally fried chicken and corn bread. I told him you were the best cook in Greene County, Mother.

I was so sorry to hear about Mrs. Schnieder's son. I certainly hope she can get the consolation from her work in the Red Cross that I have – it's the most inspiring work I ever hope to be in.

I finally received a letter from Ben. It was very nice and in it he invited me down for another visit.

P.S. The enclosed picture was taken before Christmas in Germany. I was serving on the "Golden West" that day. With me are Bunny Ronalds and Peggy Gough, Spencer Tracy's personal secretary. She quit her job to join the Red Cross. No wonder I had so much trouble getting in.

February 27, 1945
Letter #59

Dearest Folks,
We have been having plenty of excitement up here the past week – we knew almost to the day when it was going to happen. Things seem to be progressing right along so maybe it won't be too long.

I'm guessing the "it" was the crossing of the Ruhr River as documented in Mom's scrapbook. Per her records, troops crossed on 2/23, taking Jülich, and three clubmobile girls crossed in their Hillman on 2/25 – don't know if Mom was one. The remaining clubmobiles crossed on 2/28.

March 3, 1945
Letter #60
Germany

Dearest Folks,
Conditions over here have been so encouraging the past week I'm almost afraid to let myself believe it. We're all so elated over the latest developments – I guess everyone is at this

point. I wouldn't miss being in this right now for anything. Those "Krauts" are really sweating it out now. I'll keep you posted on the latest from Group C. Just keep your fingers crossed and pray that it won't be much longer.

P.S. I want to request some thyroid pills—one grain tablets. They are very difficult to obtain over here and the doctor suggested I order some from the states immediately. I have menstruated only once since coming overseas and that was in January after the thyroid treatment. My trip to

Paris at that time was taken up almost entirely with examinations and tests. The thyroid they gave me at that time worked beautifully as long as my supply held out. I reacted to the treatment very normally and started menstruating almost immediately. I have since run completely out of the medicine and now find it impossible to get at all. I wouldn't even give it a second thought if I didn't feel so "draggy" and sluggish most of the time. I imagine both Daddy and the censor are getting a big kick out of my bodily ailments at this point. Please send me a large supply as soon as possible – I'm terrible anxious to get straightened out.

Mom's condition, trending toward early onset menopause, was satisfactorily resolved before permanent damage resulted, as evidenced by the two sons she was to bear. Group C had reached the Rhine by now, passing through reclaimed München-Gladbach, home of Herr Goebbels, along the way, and arriving at Düsseldorf on March 1st. A note under a picture of the Rhine in her scrapbook reads, "First to reach the Rhine – March 1, 1945." They did not cross until March 28th, serving troops east of the river as they moved north to cross at Wesel.

March 10, 1945
Letter #61

Dearest Folks,
    Our clubmobile has been on detached service and just rejoined the outfit yesterday. I have worked harder the past few days than I have my whole stay overseas. It has been the most interesting week I have yet experienced. I guess the "Dixie Queen" and the "Lone Star" are the

first two clubmobiles to reach the Rhine – we had the privilege of seeing the famous river before it was crossed. The "Lone Star" was photographed by the Associated Press and will probably appear in the newsreel so be on the lookout. You can see where we have been and the outfit we served.

We have been moved again since I last wrote. Our new quarters are very comfortable with exception of the water situation. There is no such thing as running water in this town so we spend most of our spare time hauling it for our personal use. Five girls and me, plus the Colonel, went 30 miles yesterday to a shower-point for a shampoo and bath, the first we have had in almost two weeks.

There has been a constant drone of plane motors overhead for the past 15 minutes. It's the most beautiful sound there is over here. I hope they flatten this country out and the people with it. I have no sympathy whatsoever with a race of people who can stir up hatred and cause the misery and suffering they have. I only wish I could tell you more about our work and the experiences we are having, but censorship won't permit. I realize more every day how fortunate I am to have an opportunity to experience all of this.

They continued to move downstream along the Rhine – north – yes, downstream, to Wesel where they crossed March 28, 1945. Downstream and upstream are different in Germany in that major rivers, the Rhine, the Weser, the Elbe, all flow north into the North Sea. At the same time, the Danube, Europe's other great river, starts next door to the Rhine and wanders hundreds of miles east before dumping into the Black Sea. As in all

Looking accross the Rhine at Dussledorf on March 1, 1945

73

terrains, great rivers dictate strategy, and the German retreat was keyed to them.

At the time Mom was "seeing the famous river," a friend's father was crossing the Rhine at Remagen in one of the fiercest battles of this stage of the war. He shared his father's story as I was finishing up Mom's. On March 7, 1945, Lightning Division (78th Infantry) set out to take Ludendorff railway bridge at Remagen, just south of Bonn. German resistance was fierce, as the Rhine was their last major natural barrier of defense. Maurice (Mo) Stack fought in that brutal encounter. He was aboard the third truck to hit the bridge, the first to cross, as the other two were destroyed. He and his men slipped into the basement of a blown out church for cover. Mo Stack recounted hearing a

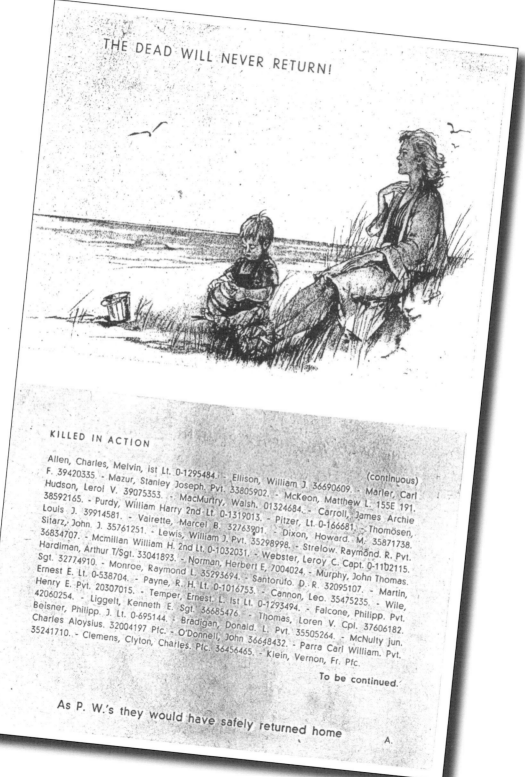

THE DEAD WILL NEVER RETURN!

KILLED IN ACTION

(continuous)

Allen, Charles, Melvin, ist Lt. 0-1295484. - Ellison, William J. 36690609. - Marler, Carl F. 39420335. - Mazur, Stanley Joseph. Pvt. 33805902. - McKeon, Matthew L. 155E 191. Hudson, Leroi V. 39075353. - MacMurtry, Walsh. 01324684. - Carroll, James Archie 38592165. - Purdy, William Harry 2nd Lt. 0-1319013. - Pitzer, Lt. 0-166681. - Thomösen, Louis J. 39914581. - Vairette, Marcel B. 32763901. - Dixon, Howard. M. 35871738. Sitarz, John. J. 35761251. - Lewis, William J. Pvt. 35298998. - Strelow. Raymond. R. Pvt. 36834707. - Mcmillan William H. 2nd Lt. 33041893. - Webster, Leroy C. Capt. 0-11b2115. Hardiman, Arthur T/Sgt. 33041893. - Norman, Herbert E. 7004024. - Murphy, John Thomas. Sgt. 32774910. - Monroe, Raymond L. 35293694. - Santorufo. D. R. 32095107. - Martin, Ernest E. Lt. 0-538704. - Payne, R. H. Lt. 0-1016753. - Cannon, Leo. 35475235. - Wile, Henry E. Pvt. 20307015. - Temper, Ernest. L. Ist Lt. 0-1293494. - Falcone, Philipp. Pvt. 42060254. - Liggelt, Kenneth E. Sgt. 36685476. - Thomas, Loren V. Cpl. 37606182. Beisner, Philipp. J. Lt. 0-695144. - Bradigan, Donald. L. Pvt. 35505264. - McNulty jun. Charles Aloysius. 32004197 Pfc. - O'Donnell, John 36648432. - Parra Carl William. Pvt. 35241710. - Clemens, Clyton, Charles. Pfc. 36456465. - Klein, Vernon, Fr. Pfc.

To be continued.

As P. W.'s they would have safely returned home

A.

74

famous BBC broadcaster, known for his "good news, bad news" reporting style, announcing the "good news that American troops had taken the bridge at Remagen" followed by the "bad news that the Germans had taken it back." "What do we do now?" a soldier had asked. "Repeat after me, Our Father who art in Heaven…" Mo Stack had responded. They shortly had to fight their way out of the church when German soldiers discovered their presence. Wonder if Mom and Mo ever met, if she was able to place a warm cup of coffee into his frostbitten hands? So many heroes, so many tales in need of telling.

March 21, 1945
Letter #63

Dearest Folks,
I am enclosing some German propaganda sheets (leaflets) dropped behind our lines. Interesting aren't they?

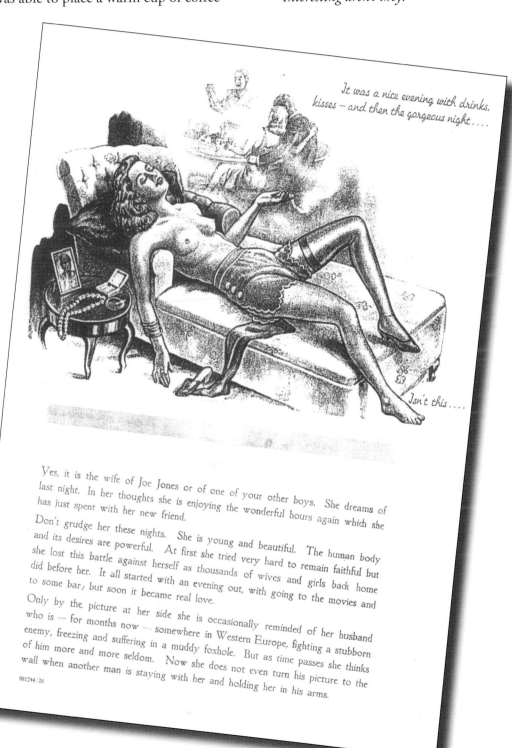

It was a nice evening with drinks, kisses — and then the gorgeous night….

Isn't this….

Yes, it is the wife of Joe Jones or of one of your other boys. She dreams of last night. In her thoughts she is enjoying the wonderful hours again which she has just spent with her new friend.
Don't grudge her these nights. She is young and beautiful. The human body and its desires are powerful. At first she tried very hard to remain faithful but she lost this battle against herself as thousands of wives and girls back home did before her. It all started with an evening out, with going to the movies and to some bar, but soon it became real love.
Only by the picture at her side she is occasionally reminded of her husband who is — for months now — somewhere in Western Europe, fighting a stubborn enemy, freezing and suffering in a muddy foxhole. But as time passes she thinks of him more and more seldom. Now she does not even turn his picture to the wall when another man is staying with her and holding her in his arms.

981244/26

We want upset,
We want War!
Please don't esk it
Just what for.

You dumb Gentiles
Kill each other,
We smart pepples
Stick to cover.

German Christians
Killing Yanks,
Whiskered rabbis
Giving thanks.

Christian sea fleets
In full sail,
Yiddish bankers
Making kale.

When the world is
Nearly damned
Then comes in our
Promised Land!

We want War, for
We make money,
You make stiffs and
Look so funny.

We take cash, for
We ain't dumb,
You take hash, and
Kingdom Come!

980245/88

Reprinted without
kind permission of
the "New Yorker".

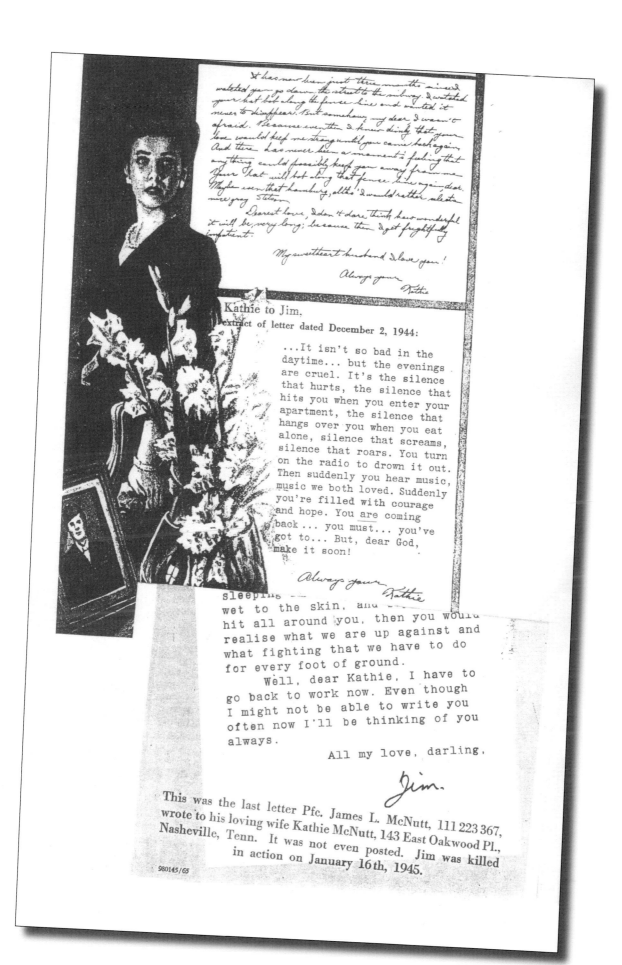

It has now been just three months since I watched you go down the street to the railway. I watched your hat bob along the fence line and wanted it never to disappear. But somehow, my dear I wasn't afraid. Because even then I knew deep in my heart that your love would keep me strong until you came back again. And there has never been a moment's feeling that anything could possibly keep you away from me. Your hat will bob along that fence line again, dear. Maybe even that hamburg, altho' I would rather see that nice gray Stetson.

Dearest love, I don't dare think how wonderful it will be; very long; because then I get frightfully impatient.

My sweetheart husband I love you!

Always your
Kathie

Kathie to Jim.

extract of letter dated December 2, 1944:

...It isn't so bad in the
daytime... but the evenings
are cruel. It's the silence
that hurts, the silence that
hits you when you enter your
apartment, the silence that
hangs over you when you eat
alone, silence that screams,
silence that roars. You turn
on the radio to drown it out.
Then suddenly you hear music,
music we both loved. Suddenly
you're filled with courage
and hope. You are coming
back ... you must... you've
got to... But, dear God,
make it soon!

Always your
Kathie

sleeping —
wet to the skin, and
hit all around you, then you would
realise what we are up against and
what fighting that we have to do
for every foot of ground.

Well, dear Kathie, I have to
go back to work now. Even though
I might not be able to write you
often now I'll be thinking of you
always.

All my love, darling,

Jim.

This was the last letter Pfc. James L. McNutt, 111 223 367,
wrote to his loving wife Kathie McNutt, 143 East Oakwood Pl.,
Nasheville, Tenn. It was not even posted. Jim was killed
in action on January 16th, 1945.

980145/65

77

FAREWELL TO DREAMS

You're fighting for home. Out here you think and dream of the bright tomorrow, of the day when you will be free to plan the future of your own.

In actual fact they are beyond interesting. They feature the expected – loneliness, broken dreams with sketches of soldiers and baby sons, infidelity keyed to innate human desire – "now she does not even turn his picture to the wall when another man is staying with her." But beyond that, the anti-Semitic slurs speak to the heart of the conflict – "German Christians killing Yanks, whiskered rabbis giving thanks. Christian sea fleets in full sail, Yiddish bankers making kale." It was only days until the horrors of Nazi preoccupation with Jews and a "final solution" at places like Auschwitz and Dachau were revealed to a stunned world.

March 26, 1945
Letter #64

Dearest Folks,
I think Katherine will love her work in the Red Cross if she really gives it a fair chance. She'll not only find it inspiring but completely absorbing. We war widows are so fortunate to have something like this to turn to.

I don't recall hearing her use that term – war widows. There were so many. I wonder how many had happy endings.

The war news is certainly encouraging. If

I had my way they wouldn't leave anything standing in this country. We'll never exterminate these people – it just isn't in us. They're going to be so sorry they ever started this thing.

Her anger runs deep. The "exterminate" word is another I never once heard her utter.

I'm sorry I never mentioned the Wentworth Memorial. I would like to make a donation in Johnnie's name. I don't feel like giving less than $100 – what do you think Daddy? You know what I think of memorials of that type, but for Johnnie's sake I think it would be a very nice gesture. I'm awfully glad you gave Ruth [Johnnie's sister] the Presidential Honorary Mention – the boys should have that. They were always so proud of their "Unk," and I would like for them to have something to remind them of him and the fine things he stood for.

April 9, 1945
Letter #68
Germany

Dearest Folks,
We have moved twice since I last wrote. I haven't even had time to read the latest "Stars and Stripes" to see how the war is progressing.

Amazing – front lines and only a whiff of success.

It has been terribly exciting around here the past six weeks – I only wish I could tell you more about it. Our billets haven't been so good the last two moves, but we're going so fast now it doesn't bother us. It won't be long now.

Guess she didn't need "Stars and Stripes" after all.

Mom crossed the Rhine at Wesel on March 28, 1945, and spoke of a town they entered called Friedrichsfeld. The write-up in her scrapbook described the Rhine bridgehead at Wesel as reminiscent of Omaha Beach, with equipment strewn all over the river bank, houses burning in town, rubble everywhere. Clubmobiles were armed for the first time, this is the Red Cross mind you, and road signs to Berlin stood out. The following two weeks they advanced through Wiedenbruck and Steinheim. On April 10, she crossed the Weser River, home to the legend of the Pied Piper of Hameln and his German rats. Along the way were refugees of all nature, some going home, some escaping from home, some with nothing, some with cadavers, some waving flags, some stumbling from malnutrition, a veritable stream of humanity seeking hope. There was no Pied Piper to lead them in this century. They would not drown, but they would have to start over again.

I couldn't help but close this chapter with a passage from the Red Cross Unit Report included in Mom's scrapbook.

Natives See Doughnuts Made
War can produce many incongruous spectacles, aided and abetted by the American Red Cross. Inhabitants of the white flagged houses of Wiedenbrück, where we moved April 5th, crowded above edges of their 17th century market square to watch the Group make doughnuts and hang out a clubmobile-to-clubmobile wash line. A sergeant in the Wehrmacht was so undone by these proceedings that he marched into the Company mess one morning and surrendered.

Oh that war could be so rational more often.

White surrender flags on laundry day

CHAPTER 10

POWs and V.E.

Franklin Delano Roosevelt died at 4:45 p.m. on April 12, 1945. It took only minutes for the news to spread around the world, though it was not until an April 16th letter that Mom reacted. The reason was work, more work than perhaps she had ever undertaken in her life. At 2 p.m. on Friday the 13th, Group C rolled into a former Luftwaffe base at Hildesheim, Germany, to serve recently released prisoners of war of all nationalities being assembled for transport home. Some arrived from the Russian front, some from the Battle of the Bulge, others from battles in north Africa and Italy. If Johnnie had survived, he might have been one. All were ill and malnourished, most with dysentery and lice.

An article in the Springfield *News-Leader* that mom had tucked into her stack of letters spoke of "thin, sallow faces" and "dull eyes." Another piece spoke of "tears rolling down dusty faces" and "gasping and weeping at the sight of American women." Raw emotion must have transcended the moment. Add FDR and the fact that a fellow Missourian was now her Commander in Chief to the mix, and I'm sure Mom's head and heart were spinning.

Purportedly, Eisenhower, Bradley and Patton, who were already severely shaken by their first encounter with a Nazi death camp [Ohrdruf-Nord] that very day, sat up much the night in Marburg, Germany, trying to sort it all out. Mom slept an exhausted sleep not far away.

April 12, 1945
Letter #68

Dearest Folks,

I want to thank you for the thyroid – it arrived in record time. I can't tell you how much it means to have some in my possession – it's scarce as hen's teeth over here. Yesterday was one of the most interesting days I have experienced in a long time. I went to a Count

Scenes from Count Metternick's estate, including a WWI grave at lower right

Metternick's estate. It was terribly run down, but still beautiful. It was completely surrounded by water and had a drawbridge at the entrance. Judging from the interior it must have been built sometime during the 18th century. There was very little furniture left, but the murals, fixtures and wallpaper showed what a handsome place it had been. The grounds looked like something you would see on an old tapestry.

Thanks again for the medicine – I'll probably be a new person within 10 days – hope so anyway.

P.S. The war news is almost too good to believe.

This was obviously written before news of FDR reached her.

Serving freed POWs at Hildeshieme

April 16, 1945
(no number)

Dearest Daddy,

It's Mother's Day soon and I hope you will take care of it for me. You have such beautiful taste and always know what she needs. All I ask is that you spend $10 or more for whatever you select.

I'm terrible sorry I haven't been better about writing lately but we have been on detached service again — this time serving our own POWs. We have been working 18 hours a day so you can see how limited my time is. I will write more about my work when I get a breathing spell, and believe me there is plenty to write about!

Roosevelt's death has been a terrible shock to everyone — I just can't get over it.

April 22, 1945
Letter #69

Dearest Folks,

We (14 girls and 3 clubmobiles) have been on detached service the past 8 days serving an ex-POW camp. We have been working 16-18 hours a day. We all have felt that this job was the highlight of our Red Cross careers. There

were 15 different nationalities represented in this camp: American, British, Canadian, Dutch, French, Polish, Chechs, Russian, Indian, Australian, New Zealand, S. African, Isle of Cyprus, Spanish, and Yugoslavs. Some of the fellows are in pretty bad shape – especially the ones captured in "the bulge." They were marched from that area to the Russian border and back into the heart of Germany again on one liter of soup (colored water) and half a slice of bread (German brown bread made up of potato peels and sawdust) a day. You can't imagine the results of months of this diet and such strenuous exercise combined. We cried when we first saw them – most of them are nothing but living skeletons. Most of them did shed tears when they first saw us – we were the first American women some of them had seen in 5 years. All of them are suffering from malnutrition which has resulted in scurvy, beriberi, TB, etc. Every one of them was covered with lice and fleas. I could go on for pages about the stories they had to tell. You

will no doubt be reading from now on about the atrocities these POWs have to relate. They can tell you things that will make your hair stand on end – they're not exaggerated either. The 8 days we were there we served over 10,000 men. Our count of donuts and coffee served the first 5 days was – 50,000 donuts and 1,180 gallons of coffee. I have taken three baths since we returned and I'm still dirty.

I met several men from the 3rd Division, but only one in the 30th Regiment. He remembered Johnnie and some of his fellow officers. J's platoon was wiped out by artillery from a German "houseboat" on the water's edge. It was later destroyed but caused them such trouble before they finally located it. This boy was captured at Anzio and last remembered Lt. Knight (who wrote the letter to mom) as commander of "K" Company. It was awfully good to know that he hadn't been killed or wounded. He recalled many of the other officers I had known. It was certainly a treat to talk with someone who knew the outfit as he did. I realize more every day how much Johnnie was spared. The majority of these fellows will never be the same – they have suffered more than anyone will ever know.

As journalist Ernie Pyle wrote in *Here Is Your War* "I don't know whether it was their good fortune or their misfortune to get out of it so early in the game. I guess it doesn't make any difference, once a man is gone."

Roosevelt's death came as a terrific shock to everyone – it made me sick. The majority of the fellows feel that they have lost not only a great leader but also a personal friend. What do you think of Truman – everyone seems a bit dubious about him. I'll be interested in your reaction to this whole affair.

Must close for now. This is terribly disconnected but I'm still living in a state of confusion, and probably will until I come home.

This letter marks the first time Mom felt at ease sharing much detail about the war she was fighting. It was as if a sense of victory had superceded concerns over censorship. I was also struck by the reference to patrician President Roosevelt as a personal friend to the common men in the trenches – a touch that propelled him to four presidential election victories.

A letter of a later date, May 31, 1945, from my grandfather bears referencing here.

Private John J. Schessler, Jr.
345 G Street
Lincoln, Nebraska

Dear Sir:

Mrs. Hogg and I were very much thrilled to receive your wonderful letter of May 28 telling us about meeting our daughter, Jean near Hildeshieme, Germany. I know it must have been a big thrill to you and the other boys when you were liberated from the German prison camps.

Dr. Toback, family and mansion

We hope that you were not too badly mistreated and that after a few weeks rest at home that you will be none the worse for your experience. I see by the morning paper that the Red Cross states that over 90% of our prisoners survived because the United States adhered strictly to the rules governing war prisoners in its hands as laid down by the Geneva Conference. It was sometimes difficult for the people here at home to understand why we treated the German prisoners so well when we knew that they were not treating our own boys in their hands equally as

well. The fact remains however that if we had mistreated the German prisoners, our own boys would have faired much worse at the hands of the Germans.

We have told Jean about your nice letter and when she gets back to the states I'm sure she will be glad to write you.

Mrs. Hogg and I both join in asking God's blessings on you and all the other brave boys who have suffered so for our beloved country, and again we want to say thanks for your nice letter.

Cordially, J. W. Hogg

Another touched by Mom – wish I could have read his letter.

April 25, 1945
Letter #70

Dearest Folks,
I'm glad you feel as you do about Truman. I actually know very little about him. Everyone has such a pessimistic attitude about him. I think they could at least give him a chance.
It's still hard to believe that Roosevelt is gone – the majority of the soldiers have taken it pretty hard. He was such a wonderful person in every way – a thoroughbred thru and thru.

April 30, 1945
Letter #71

Dearest Folks,
We are on detached service again and as busy as ever. Our work is very interesting, but not as inspiring as our last assignment – nothing will ever touch that.
We received a directive from headquarters stating that the only R.C. personnel eligible for transfer (either to the states or another theater of operations) are those who have served 2 years or more overseas. I had hoped to transfer to the Pacific, but I'm afraid I came over a year too late for that. Oh well, I'm happy just to be serving in any way I can. I will never stop being thankful to you all for making all of this possible for me. I consider it the greatest privilege in the world to be with and serve our fighting men.

As best I can tell from Mom's scrapbook, the detached service referenced above involved serving the Commanding General's Mess of the 8th Armored Division from April 22 to April 27 at an unnamed village in the Harz Mountains. The scrapbook features poignant pictures of Mom dancing with a GI in the street while local villagers looked on in seemingly stunned silence. She scribbled in the margin that "the Harz Mountains are the legendary home of German Gods … where witches

are still reported to fly and werewolves howl." She also included photos of a Dr. Toback in full military dress and in whose mansion they resided for several days. She indicated the family was caught by surprise and rushed out of the house with children, leaving dirty plates on the table and family photos scattered about. She confessed to funny feelings about the circumstances and the place. Not sure why it didn't make her letters, perhaps because of the pace of events.

And, then it was over. On May 7, 1945, the Nazis were vanquished, although victory could not be announced until the following morning to gain Stalin's concurrence.

May 8, 1945 – V-E Day. I think it sneaked up on Mom, if not the world. Russians and American troops met at the Elbe in late April. Mussolini was hanged by his countrymen April 28. Hitler killed himself May 1. The Red Army took Berlin May 2. Has there ever been a week like that in our world? The good guys (most of whom lived west of the Rhine) won. The bad guys (Stalin) won. The worst guys (Nazis) lost. The good guys joined up with the best of the worst guys and fought the bad guys in a war of nuclear bluffing and arrogance for the next half century.

May 11, 1945
Letter #73

Dearest Folks,
This has been one of the most exiting weeks of my life. We knew almost the minute peace was declared – even before it was officially announced. It's the most wonderful feeling in the world to know that there won't be any more lives lost over here.

I cried when reading this for the first time – inexplicably, quietly, in solitude. I cannot name the emotion. Her wording was neither profound nor prophetic. It was in fact quite simple. Perhaps it was sharing the moment of triumph as she recorded it for those closest too her. Maybe it was gratitude that she would be OK, that she would come home to have and love me as she loved those to whom she wrote those words. I will never know what she felt on May 7. I can only imagine. Wonder what the other most exciting weeks

of her life were. Probably the week she got married to her childhood sweetheart whose untimely death led her to that place and time. Probably the week she shipped out from Washington D.C. having bucked odds and age requirements to seek redemption from grief among brave souls risking life and limb to restore order to a world gone mad. I truly don't know why I leaked, but it was real, the emotion I felt reading that phrase, the love and admiration I felt for my mom.

She later stated in an interview with the Springfield *News-Leader* on the 50th anniversary of V-E Day that "The sun was shining … it

was real pretty." She didn't remember exactly how the word came to her, only that "It was busy. We were serving the troops, pouring coffee, handing out doughnuts we'd made, exchanging small talk with tired soldiers near Magdeburg, Germany, 75 miles west of Berlin. Everybody was just ecstatic. It was a wonderful feeling."

We all realize that there is still a big job to be done. We don't know yet what part we will play. I would still like to go to the Pacific, but I guess I'm needed over here worse than I am there. I won't even think about seeing you all again for at least another year. If the time goes as fast as it has, it won't be long. This past year has been so wonderful and exciting. I wouldn't take anything for it. I almost feel selfish for the worry and concern I must have caused you all. You both have been wonderful about the whole thing, and I can't thank you enough for your unselfishness.

We have moved again since I last wrote – this time approximately 250 miles. We started at 10:30 a.m. one morning and didn't reach our destination until 1:00 a.m. the next morning.

As best I can determine this 14-hour trek was from Oschersleben to Friedberg, a distance comparable to what it had taken the past month to cover and serve.

Driving a GMC clubmobile that distance is no fun – we were all really "pooped out" from it. I hope my next long trip like that will be from Washington, D.C to Springfield, MO.!

P.S. One of our air corps officers flew me up to the Elbe the other day. I could actually see our guns firing at the Germans across the river. It was quite an experience.

Mom later elaborated on that visit to her grandson Patrick. She told him that she had joined a small group of U.S. and Russian troops at the Elbe, and skoaled vodka with them. She remembered thinking "they are going to take me home on a gurney!" She also recalled the Russians "as very rough." She named the date to be April 25, 1945, just before war's end.

May 15, 1945
Letter #74
Dearest Folks,
*   Our group had quite an exciting experience last Saturday. We received an invitation to attend the 12th Army Group victory dance given in honor of General Bradley. It was over a 100 mile drive from where we are now (Friedberg)*

and all transportation was furnished by them (7 beautiful sedans).

While we were waiting to go through the receiving line whom should I run into but Maj. Bud Dark - what a grand reunion it was! It was a very elegant party with enough stars represented to fill the sky. Gen. Bradley looks just like his pictures and has that soft Missouri accent. Bud and I talked with him about our state. We were also honored with Marlene Dietrich's presence. She looked very lovely, much more attractive off screen than on.

I had another pleasant surprise. Whom should I meet but Capt. Paul Dougherty, one of

Johnnie's
best friends.
He knew all about
Johnnie – in fact he was an
eyewitness to the whole thing. Their
companies were side by side and his happened
to be the lucky one.

The whole thing was unnecessary – they blindly walked into a trap. Lt. Knight (who wrote the "Johnnie" letter to Mom) was killed in Italy also – just outside Cassino. I won't go into detail, but it was very sad. Paul himself looks much older and very nervous. This isn't very lifting information, but thought you might be interested. War is so horrible and ugly – I just pray to God we never have another one. I shall never forget the sweet note Lt. Knight wrote me – I only hope someone did the same for his wife.

You will find a map showing our present location. All censorship has been lifted according to the latest directive.

Next
was a Mother's
Day card with a kindly
looking gray-haired, eye-glass
rimmed mother and a GI. Only this GI was given Mom's curly brown hair and ARC uniform to personalize her message. Guess there wasn't much demand for Mother-Daughter cards in Friedberg those days. She followed that with Letter #75 to her Mom asking for help with Father's Day. No matter what her words about further service, I sensed she was getting homesick.

May 20, 1945
Letter #76

Dearest Folks,

The group moved from Friedberg to Bad-Nauheim while were away on detached service. This is such a wonderful set-up in every respect it's almost too good to be true. We're residing in a beautiful hotel with all modern conveniences. You don't know what a treat it is to be billeted in a place that has running water – hot and cold at that.

This is a very trying time for the boys, as you can well imagine. All they can think and talk about is who is eligible for that final trip home.

We don't know yet what the future holds for us or clubmobiling. We'll be going on detached service from now on because the units are so scattered out. We went thru Frankfurt yesterday on a return trip. It must have been a beautiful city at one time, but now it's about as badly destroyed as Aachen. It's going to take years to rebuild this country.

My next letter will undoubtedly be written from Cannes – so until then.

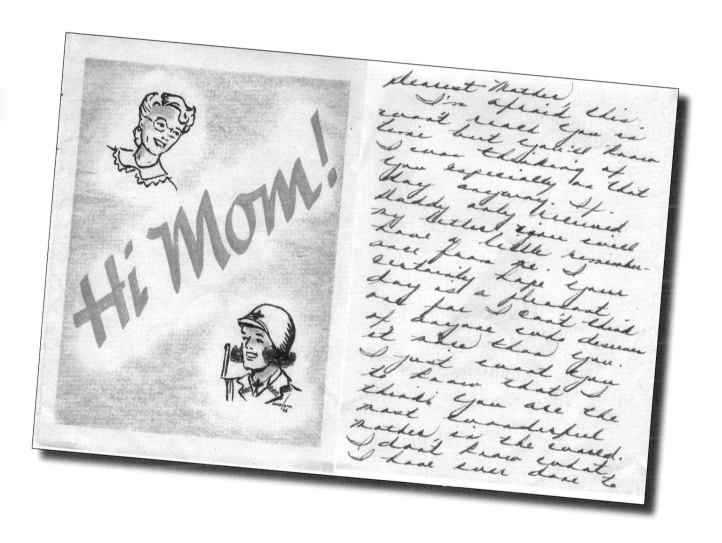

93

CHAPTER 11

Winding Down

The hard part for Mom was over. Yet, I read with interest of the wind down, the change in focus and even direction. She had been at war for six months, in the middle of it all, comforting and inspiring "the boys" who turned the tide of history. I include these last letters to bring closure, to share Mom's frame of mind as she turned down the backstretch for home.

May 25, 1945
Letter #77
Cannes, France

Dearest Folks,
 As you can see from the letterhead, I finally made it to the Riviera.
 We flew over a section of the Alps which are indescribable with their snow capped beauty and vastness. At one point we were at 9,000 feet and I thought my eardrums would burst.
 We flew over the Isle of Corsica and Cannes a couple of times before landing but the most beautiful sight of all was the Mediterranean

from the air. I can certainly appreciate Johnnie's description of it now. It's the most beautiful shade of blue – so peaceful.

May 31, 1945
Letter #78
Cannes, France

Dearest Folks,
  This is our last day at the Riviera. We have had permanents, facials, and manicures. There are about five men to every woman down here.

Funny she had never commented on the ratio before, particularly when it was 5000 to 1 on the front lines.

  I had hoped to get to Monte Carlo while here, but it's "off limits" to Americans. I realize that this restriction is for our own good, but it is terrible disappointing.

June 3, 1945
(Numbering of letters ceased at this point,

ending with #78.)
Germany

Dearest Folks,
  It's good to be back and ready to go to work again. It is possible that by the time our next leave comes (Sept) air transportation to the states will be open and we can take our seven days there. You can certainly depend on seeing me about then if it does!
  You can see that my future is about as unsettled as the weather. We probably won't know anything definite until fall. This type of work isn't much of a challenge to one's intelligence, but it is so inspiring. I don't know how the clubmobiles themselves are going to stand up under the strain another year – they have had far more wear and tear than their crews. They are a wonderful truck – I'll never cease to marvel at their endurance. They are our babies and we'll always love them. So much has happened this past year it doesn't seem possible that I left home 12 months ago. I have missed being with you and Daddy more than you'll ever know. Thank you both for letting me come.
  All my love to you both – Jeannie Bug

June 10, 1945
Germany

Dearest Folks,
  We're serving the troops again and are making such long drives we meet ourselves coming. Now that the war is over the officers are much more demanding. I never was much of a party gal and still "ain't." I love serving the troops but hate the other. I hope I don't sound like a "prig" when I say I don't like these drunken brawls some of the officers throw. Practically everyone over here drinks to excess. I honestly think we're going to have a serious problem on our hands unless a great transformation takes place.

This is really Mom's only reference to "problems" with the "boys" in all of her letters. She did share one unpleasant encounter earlier in the war. Seems that one of Dad's LSU fraternity brothers came on to her during an R&R visit to Belgium from Aachen. He lured her to his room to share pictures, pushed her onto the bed, locked the door and moved toward her. She remembers her intense anger. She expressed it by kicking him across the room with both legs. "You sorry SOB, get me out of this room or I will scream." Mom has always been able to take care of herself.

An article appeared in the Springfield paper shortly thereafter with a bizarre picture of soldiers, mine-sweep-

ers, and bathing suit clad Red Cross ladies. Posed is an understatement for this photo.

It was awfully sweet of the little boy from Nebraska to write you. He is a perfect example of the type man we served our eight days at Hildeshiem. They were such a fine group of young men with so much courage and determination.

LEARN ABOUT MINES— Two Yank soldiers demonstrate how they proceed the Riviera area of France. The audience consists of Red Cross clubmobile girls, who served in Germany and now are resting at the famed resort. One of the interested girls is Mrs. Jean H. Rayl, Springfield, second girl from the left in this picture. Mrs. Rayl, who has been overseas a year, is the former Miss Jean Hogg, daughter of Mr. and Mrs. J. Wyman Hogg, 1125 Benton. Her husband, Lt. John H. Rayl, was killed in action during the Sicilian campaign in August, 1943.
—*Associated Press Wirephoto*

Mom is actually the first girl on the left.
The newspaper is in error.

96

It is obviously this soldierly profile that stuck with her over the years.

I was invited to attend an operetta given by some Polish girls. We learned that they were Polish guerillas who had fought in the defense of Warsaw. The majority of them were from wealthy Polish families and highly educated. I was the only American woman present and as much of a curiosity to them as they were to me. I was afraid I would have to carry my hand in a sling the next day after shaking hands with all (60) of them – such strength I have never seen.

It was in this letter dated June 22, 1945, from Bad Nauheim, Germany, that she described the contents of a box forwarded previously. Included were gifts, flags, and memorabilia. "The miscellaneous items are just junk I stuck in to fill up space. The china pipe was a gift from one of the POWs I met at Hildeshiem. He carried it with him the whole time he was a prisoner – he insisted I take it." So the fragile three-piece pipe in her ammo box was china, and had been carried gently for months through a captured soldier's living hell. I went back to the box and held it again. It still smelled of tobacco and featured a peaceful scene with two deer painted on the bowl. Maybe it had comforted him through his travail. Whatever – it now bore more meaning for me. That he gave it to a perfect stranger after having been served coffee and doughnuts by her speaks to something, though I can't quite name it.

June 29, 1945
Bad Nauheim, Germany

Dearest Folks,
I could have flown over to Sicily from Cannes if I had been determined enough. I did want to visit Italy, but have no desire to go to Sicily. It's

not that I am afraid – I just want to remember Johnnie as I last saw him.

July 6, 1945
Bad Nauheim, Germany

Dearest Folks,

This week has been a hectic one with Clubmobile "C" splitting up. The group has been divided into two sections since Dec., but that hasn't kept us from being together. Yesterday we learned from HQ that one of our sections is to leave the corps within 10 days and be permanently assigned to another division. Our section will stay in Bad Nauheim. This group has been together for almost a year and it hurts terribly to see it broken up. It looked for a while as though the corps we are serving would be sent to the Pacific – had that been the case, Group C would have gone right along with them. Fate is against me going to the Pacific.

You're all I have left in this world and don't

forget it! You have been my living inspiration to carry on and try to make something of myself. I may have failed, but I have at least tried. Just remember that I love you both more than anything.

July 10, 1945
Bad Nauheim, Germany

Dearest Folks,

The past two days have been more like a glorious weekend at home. Sunday morning I sang in the choir and spent the afternoon on the golf course. We have been unable to obtain balls so it's every man for himself. I have managed to pick up three at various places and am guarding them with my life.

There is a wonderful circus playing over in Friedberg and I got to see that last night. It's sort of an international affair with practically every nationality represented but Germans. They're using the "Krauts" for cleaning up after the animals. This circus was stranded over here

when war broke out and have been here ever since. They have been giving two performances a day for the past week. All they're asking for their services is food for themselves and their animals – sort of pitiful isn't it? They are real artists.

July 15, 1945
Bad Nauheim, Germany

Dearest Folks,
Just a year ago today we left the U.S. bound for Europe on the Queen Elizabeth. I shall never forget it if I live to be a hundred. Too much has happened since then it seems very insignificant now.

July 20, 1945
Bad Nauheim, Germany

Dearest Folks,
There has been so much excitement around here. I went to Wiesbaden to see Nance and Dugal and attend their Sect. Captain's wedding. There was a lovely reception afterwards with much brass in evidence. Among those present was none other than Gen. Bradley himself – looking just as cute as ever. He seemed to be in much higher spirits than he was at the Victory Ball – guess the trip home was what he needed. I asked him how Missouri looked and he replied "It looked wonderful the three days I was there, but boy was it hot." Later in the afternoon I was fortunate enough to have my picture taken with him. Someone suggested that all of the Missourians get together – there were 2 GI's, 4 R.C. girls, and Gen Bradley. I would certainly love a copy of that but doubt I'll ever even see one. It was great fun for everyone – he's such a wonderful sport and so very democratic.

One of the R.C. girls in the picture was Mary "Chi Chi" Metcalfe, Clubmobile Group A, whose husband "Rex" Rexford later wrote an entertaining account of her tour of duty.

Speaking of Dugal reminds me of a very unusual incident that took place on her clubmobile the other day. They, like all other groups, have insignia and the names of the crew members plus their home state printed on the outside of their clubmobile. They happen to have a "Mary from Missouri" on their truck. They were parked in the middle of a little German town serving one day when up walked a German woman inquiring about "Mary from Mo." They informed her that Mary had gone back to the states – St. Louis whereupon she retorted with "My home was in Missouri – Springfield." Dugal was floored with this response, but continued the conversation by telling her that she had a very good friend over here in R.C. from that city. To make a long story short this woman knew both the Rayls and the Hoggs. In fact she was an employee of Daddy's at one time. She mentioned the fact that Daddy was in the loan business, and that she had worked for him back in the middle

30's. She left Springfield in '39 and married some German diplomat in Washington. He was forced to return to Germany shortly thereafter and she naturally went with him. She was a very haggard looking woman in her early 40s. She had at least eight children hanging on to her apron strings and one in arm – all for "der Fatherland," I presume. She spoke longingly of Missouri and remarked that she hoped to return some day. Dugal was so dumfounded at this point that she forgot to get her name.

Guess I'd better close for now – we have a big serving day tomorrow.

Even then, the world was small.

July 27, 1945
Bad Nauheim, Germany

Dearest folks,
You'll be pleased to hear that I have had the rare opportunity of seeing our own President

Eisenhower, Hickey Greet President

President Truman chats with Brig. Gen. Doyle O. Hickey, left, commanding general of the Third Armored Div. and Gen. Eisenhower before reviewing troops of the Spearhead Div. yesterday morning.

President Truman Looks Over
2 Divisions in Frankfurt Area

Truman, Sect. Of State, and General Eisenhower since I last wrote. Truman and his party flew down from Berlin yesterday (between sessions with Stalin and Churchill), and arrived at Frankfort around 8:30 a.m. We were scheduled to serve the air-strip later that morning and the early part of the afternoon. When we heard they were leaving that afternoon around 4:00, we decided to stay in spite of the crowd and terrific heat. While waiting for the final departure, four of us went thru the President's famous plane (the Sacred Cow). It is a C-54, the interior of which was designed for Roosevelt. Unfortunately, he only had one flight in it after it was completed. It is very luxuriously finished – complete with kitchen, lounge, elevator, etc. I imagine Roosevelt's physical handicap accounts for the elevator. The floor and passageway are covered with beautiful beige carpet with drapes to match.

This, by the way, is not for publication

since no one but the President, his party, and the guards are allowed within 50 ft. of it. We "vamped" the guards into letting us have a quick "gander," otherwise we would have never had such an experience. Red Cross girls get by with murder over here!

We returned to stand on the sideline and watched the whole performance. Truman reviewed the 42nd Airborne Div., presented

awards, and made a brief speech while the SHEAF band played in the background. Truman wore a pearl-gray suit, Eisenhower his suntan dress uniform and Byrnes navy blue. At one time we were not more than 10 feet from the party – in fact, we were so close that even I could see their features. We then watched them board their planes and take off for Berlin. We all but died of a heat stroke before it was over, but it was well worth it!

Mom says her friends urged her to walk up to President Truman and introduce herself as a fellow Missourian – guess you could do that back then. "Just too shy" she concludes.

August 2, 1945
Bad Nauheim, Germany

Dearest Folks,
This marks another anniversary that you no doubt recall as well as I. These last two years have passed rather quickly, much to my

amazement. I was on my way to Plymouth for my first assignment this time last year. Maybe '46 will find us all together.

August 6, 1945
Bad Nauheim, Germany

Everyone over here is so excited over the latest war news – this new atomic bomb may bring things to an end much sooner than anticipated.

Note the date – how could she know so quickly?
Then, just when Mom thought it was over, a rare letter in the stack "from" instead of "to" her mother. Because of a change in Mom's mailing address, it arrived August 9, which is why I have placed it here in the chronology.

July 25, 1945

Dearest Jeannie,
It's very hard for me to write what I'm going to

have to – Brother was killed last night – the #3
engine blew up and blew his plane to bits.

"Brother" was one of Mom's childhood friends, Forrest Nichols, the closest to a brother she had. His leather flight jacket hangs in our closet yet today, a gift from his folks to Mom, from her to me. I never knew much about it. I pulled it out upon reading this letter – "krachy kourier" was the nickname emblazoned on the front. Stitched inside was an American flag, with what appeared to be Arabic and Chinese writing underneath – hard to figure. Each shoulder carried a patch, as did the left chest, a fire-breathing serpent with red wings. It is in remarkably good state.

> *I know how this news is going to hurt you.*
> *I wish I could be there to share this sorrow*
> *with you.*
> *You recall how he had to conquer that sickness*
> *at the beginning of his flying career. Then he*
> *came back with all those missions to his credit*
> *(67), and the Army wanted to make him an*
> *instructor – he just wouldn't be anything but*
> *a combat flier.*

This letter, and a subsequent one, takes on a different

tone after a sharing of facts. My Grandmother's pent-up anxiety and anger begin to direct the pen.

> *You may think it ignorant and superstitious, but I actually believe it is fatal to force the events of one's life. Remember how Johnnie had the safe places in HQ, and how he just would get into the thick of action. And now I'm applying this to you honey — you trying to force your way into more dangerous work. Please Jeannie, don't try to go on to the Pacific. I've tried to be brave and let you live your own life — Daddy and I have tried every minute to hold the best thoughts for your safety and to encourage you in this wonderful work you are doing — but, we've had about all we can take.*
>
> *How I do hate to have to write to you of such sad things —*
>
> *All my love, Mom*
> *July 26, 1945*

> *Dearest Jeannie,*
> *No doubt you are thinking your mother is a*

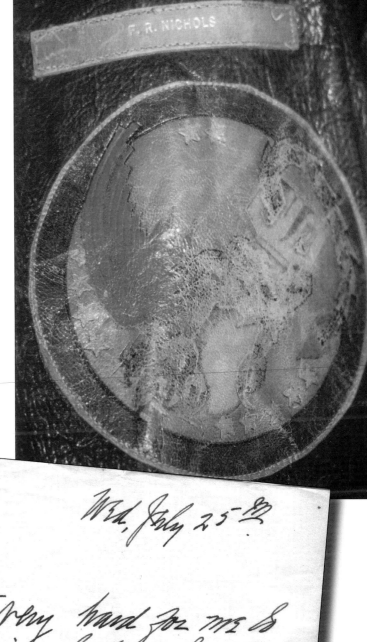

Wed, July 25th

Dearest Jeannie,

It's very hard for me to write what I'm going to have to. Brother was killed last night. The #3 engine blew up & blew his plane to bits — those in the front of the plane were blown out. Five parachuted to safety. This blow seems al—

selfish, demanding woman because I said what I did in yesterday's letter about you going to the Pacific. As I told you in that letter, I can clearly see where Johnnie and Brother both defied "fate." Johnnie was determined to move into combat. I believe now that is why he found it hard to get along with his C.O. when he was in H.Q. He didn't even try to be content with his work there. And that was the way Brother was about his instructing job. You are possessed by the same urge that made these boys work themselves into those dangerous positions. The Lord has been with you honey, all the past months – don't disregard his loving care and go thrusting yourself into new dangers. I know you have braved plenty of hardship and dangers over where you are and there have been times you could have been killed. I've not said this before because I know you resent being dramatized. I hate that too, but I have to bring it up now. It is just that I know you have risked enough and endured enough.

Try to bear with me if I seem selfish and demanding. Daddy and I love you so much.

My grandmother's emotional full court press worked, and Mom's efforts to switch war theatres ceased.

August 10, 1945
Bad Nauheim, Germany

Dearest folks,
Your two letters of yesterday dated July 25th and July 26th just knocked me off my "props." Aside from Johnnie's death I don't know when anything has shocked or hurt as much as this horrible news of Brother. I couldn't feel any worse if I had lost my own brother. I went all to pieces when I read your letter – can't seem to pull myself together enough to write his family. It's so hard to understand why such things must happen.

I think we all have had as much of this war as we can take. Thank God the end is in sight! Just like you Mother, I haven't allowed myself to think of the dangers involved in this work these past months.

I don't think you need to worry about my going to the Pacific, as rapidly as the war is progressing over there. I realize now how selfish it was of me not to consider you all first. Young people are so "pig-headed" and self-centered they can't see past their nose. I will admit now that I pulled every string in the Red Cross to get over there after V-E Day, but to no avail. I promise right now that I will dismiss it from my mind if it will give you some peace of mind. Forgive me for being so thoughtless – I have already given you more than your share of anxiety.

August 15, 1945
Bad Nauheim, Germany

Dearest Folks,
Happy "V-J" Day! We received the wonderful news this morning over the BBC. Everyone is still in a daze – the same one they have been in since the first atomic bomb was dropped and Japan's immediate surrender became inevitable. It's still hard to believe the war is actually over after almost four years of it. Little did we realize what an eventful year 1945 would be – total victory and the world at peace in three months time. It's almost too good to be true isn't it?

I have hardly been myself since the tragic news arrived. The Nichols have always been like a second family to Mary and me – Billy and Brother were the first children Mary and I played with. It's such a pity that it had to happen so near the end. Those of us that are left behind are the sufferers. It's up to us to carry on so that the generations to come won't have to know the horrors of war.

There is a possibility that I may be coming home next spring. It depends entirely on the amount of troops the Army is able to send home from this theater within the next six months. The R.C. is going to need less personnel in this theater as time goes on. We all feel that clubmobile will be extinct by Christmas – I hope not! My 18 months of overseas service will be up in January. I want to stay as long as I'm needed.

August 20, 1945
Bad Nauheim, Germany

Dearest folks,

I don't know any more about my future right now than you do, but until I do I plan to settle down with my own Mom and Dad if they don't object. I think I have had enough adventure the past 14 months to last me a lifetime.

I feel just the same toward matrimony as I did when I left home – you can't go right out and find just the right person like you would select choice fruit or vegetables. You know that I haven't closed my mind to that sort of thing, but at the same time I'm not just looking for someone to take care of me the rest of my life.

I was happily married once myself and I'll be damned if I'm going to be rushed into something I don't want.

Mom married Dad 353 days later – choice fruit or vegetable?

Saturday was an exciting day for us – we served the Bob Hope Show. After the show we took care of 8,000 troops – our largest serving since Hildeshieme. The show was wonderful – it's the type of entertainment the troops need. Poor Bob is beginning to show his age – no wonder!

August 26, 1945
Bad Nauheim, Germany

Dearest Folks,

We have been terrible busy getting ready to move – this time to Friedberg (our old stomping grounds). It isn't more than 3 miles from Bad Nauheim, but as much trouble as a move across the country. Fifteenth Army is taking over "B.N." to write the history of the war. The town isn't large enough for both of us, if you know what I mean. R.C. headquarters wants us to get out "PDQ," and we are!

Serving the troops with a headless Bob Hope.

September 3, 1945
Bad Nauheim, Germany

Dearest Folks,

We're not living as luxuriously as we were in Bad Nauheim, but have ten times more privacy. I'm sure we will be more comfortable this winter – the house is small and will be easy to heat.

Monday night we had an emergency call from H.Q. in Wiesbaden. It seems that there had been a very bad troop train wreck about 80 miles south of us. They wanted every available girl as soon as possible. We loaded the clubmobiles with supplies and were on the road by midnight. We reached our destination around 1:45 a.m. In other words, we drove 80 miles in an hour and 50 minutes – record-breaking time in those trucks. We were then informed it was a false alarm. There was nothing to do but turn around and head for home. We were all nearly dead when we arrived in Friedberg around 5:30 that morning. My crew is on leave, so I had to drive that "blasted" truck both ways!

My chances for coming home next spring are just that much better. I feel certain I'll be ready by then. Do you think I am terrible to want to come home at the end of my 18 months? Remember how I wanted to make a career of it when I joined? The picture has changed so much since then, or maybe I have. I am interested in but one thing – going home!

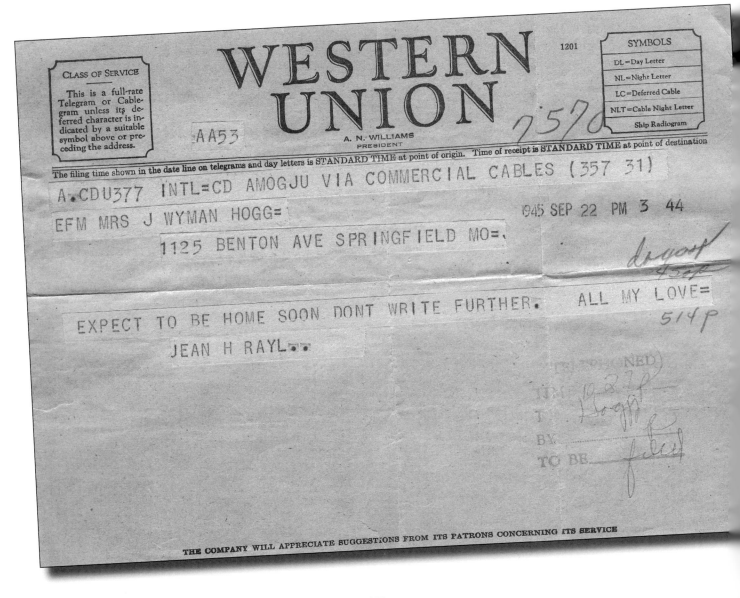

September 11, 1945
Friedberg, Germany

Dearest Folks,

Effective next week, I lose my job on the "Dixie Queen" and become captain of the club-mobile "Yosemite." After three months of trial captaincy my salary will increase from $150 to $175 a month. This is no particular honor – there just wasn't anyone left to take over!

And then, out of the blue....

September 13, 1945
Friedberg, Germany

Dearest Folks,

This is just to let you know that I am leaving Germany this Sunday for Paris for final clearing to come home.

I can't imagine what reading that sentence must have meant to my grandparents.

This is as much of a surprise to me as it is to you – in fact, I can hardly hold the pen. I'm so excited! They are releasing girls by hundreds. Don't worry, I wasn't fired! I volunteered to come home. I have been rather homesick lately and thought it best to take advantage of the shipping space right now. Heaven only knows how long the processing will take in Paris. Until you hear from me again either by letter or plane.

All my love to you both, Jeannie Bug

And then the last one, the last letter in the box.

September 19, 1945
Paris, France

Dearest Daddy,

I hope the letter I sent several days ago advising you of my return to the USA within the month arrived. I will be in Paris processing

109

SOUVENIR ISSUE
OCT. 9. 1945

JOHN ERICSSON

WELCOME HOME

SEAWEED GAZETTE

The faint outline of the Statue of
Liberty welcomes Mom home.

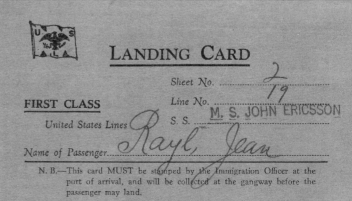

LANDING CARD

Sheet No. _2_

FIRST CLASS

United States Lines

Line No. _19_

S.S. _M. S. JOHN ERICSSON_

Name of Passenger _Rayl, Jean_

N. B.—This card MUST be stamped by the Immigration Officer at the
port of arrival, and will be collected at the gangway before the
passenger may land.

M-6610

until the first of next week. At this rate, don't be expecting that call from New York until the middle of October.

There were a couple of Western Union cables to 1125 S. Benton, the last dated September 30, 4:38 p.m. announcing "ARRIVING NEW YORK JOHN ERICSSON MIDDLE OCTOBER," and then it was over. 430 days after leaving New York harbor, Mom was headed home.

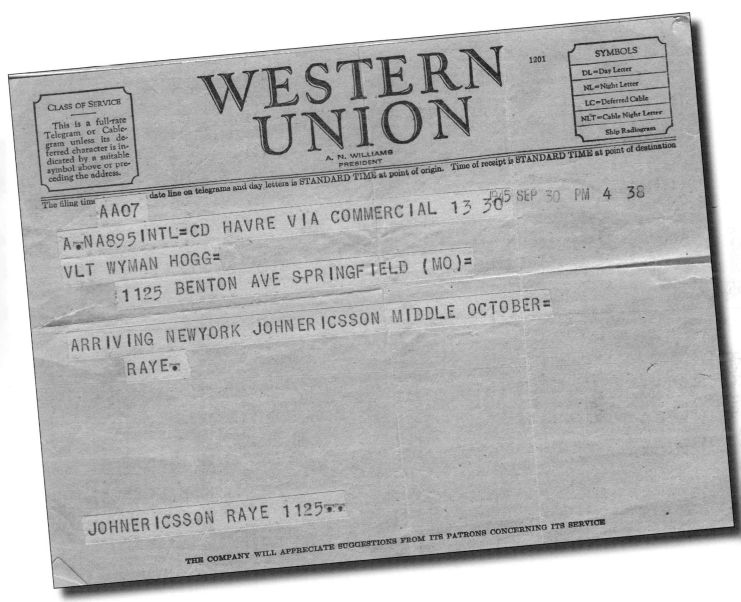

CHAPTER 12

Everafter

Supply of letters exhausted, all that remained was the scrapbook, the focus of which moved to reunions. One picture, undated, shows 13 women out of the 30 listed in Group "C's" original roster. They appear in varying sizes and shades of gray. My guess is 1970, a twenty-fifth anniversary gathering. Mom can't recall. I only know she looks fit and fresh, and happy to be there.

A second set of pictures relates to a 50th anniversary of D-Day event, held at St. Louis's University Club on June 4, 1994, in the President's Room. The menu featured "Victory Garden Salad" and "Liberated French Pastries." The invitation called for veterans in uniform or vintage clothing. Mom wore hers.

A picture of Mom and "Chichi" Metcalfe Rexford, hats cocked, fully adorned, in front of an American flagged bandstand, wearing smiles as big as the stage itself, speaks volumes about brave women. Ironically, friends of ours were having dinner in an adjoining room, and stuck their heads in to pay tribute to local veterans. John Schnoebelen called early next morning to announce that he had met a most amazing woman

the previous evening. Now John is a faithful and loyal husband and I was a little taken aback by his enthusiasm for a lady other than his wife Joan. He described this woman as "a little older" but full of spirit and optimism, and repeated their conversation, which included "You know Todd Parnell? Why, he's my son!" He said Mom "sparkled" throughout the evening.

I also came upon an ARC Clubmobile Group "C" publication, POOP SHEET, Vol. VIII, No. 1, December 1957. It contained correspondence from almost all of Mom's compatriots, ranging from bragging on husbands and kids, to travels, to health conditions. Mom's letter stated "I can hardly wait to receive the 'poop from the group' this year as always. It brings back so many fond memories along with making me very homesick to see everyone. The welcome mat is always out for anyone passing thru the Ozarks. May 1958 be the best year of all."

So there it is – little in the way of blood and guts, though she saw plenty of both.

It seems apparent to me that in Mom's moments of greatest peril, say bombed out hotels or the Battle of the Bulge, she shared the least. Beyond security concerns, there is almost a protective reflex for parents and friends. No sensationalism in her reporting from the front.

Her story is a tale of courage, and of love. We've focused on the courage part – what's love got to do with it? I got a father for starters. It is highly unlikely that my mother and father would have seen the light of each other without war.

Beyond that, I've noticed that I have become more attentive to the "stories" since beginning this endeavor, and so many of them are love stories. World War II spawned the biggest baby boom in our country's short history. Demographically speaking, these births are still defining our future, although most of the "spawners"

are gone. Not all these births were love children, but many were as our nation poured out its collective tears and emotions in an historic wave of baby-making. Love has at lot to do with it – Mom's, and our nation's, post-war story.

Several months ago, I rode down the elevator in my parents' condominium building with an elderly couple, just the three of us on a fifteen-floor journey. They were holding hands and smiling. After a moment of hesitation, she said, "He was released from prison camp 57 years ago today." That would have been April 29, 1945, just as Mom was serving freed prisoners of war in the heart of the German countryside. "We married 56 years ago this coming June 30. I waited for him." He blushed slightly. She beamed. That's a love story.

Driving to work shortly thereafter, NPR reported the 60th anniversary of "Rosie the Riveter." This national campaign to mobilize women into the workforce after Pearl Harbor was a stunning success, and a precursor to today's professional women. Prior to 1942, women in

general stayed home and raised the babies. World War II changed that forever, although the stereotype died hard. One of the "Rosies" reported that she lied about her age and went to work in Los Angeles on C-147s just after her 15th birthday. She described in detail the precision of her labors, sometimes ripping out rivets and replacing them in the interest of perfection. She also discussed hiding handwritten notes in the planes as they rolled off the assembly line – things like "We miss you boys," "Come home safe and soon," "We are proud of our brave soldiers." One such note was discovered by a young paratrooper as he prepared to jump. He kept it, and at a post-war gathering struck up a conversation with a young lady, who soon confessed to planting the very message of encouragement he had received. They were soon married, and remain so. That's a love story.

Mom and Dad, after 56 years together – that's a love story too.

This project came to mind one cold Veteran's Day

several years ago as Mom and I stood next to her parents' gravesite. She remarked that she had been driving across Europe in a truck at that very time some 50 years earlier. Later that day at her house, she expanded on her wartime experiences. She opened up her scrapbook and handed over "the Box." Every tale she shared that day was confirmed in her letters or scrapbook, save one, which she mentioned to grandson Patrick as he was trying to wrestle additional details from her failing memory. She talked to him about Dachau. She had no pictures, made no mention in her letters. She told him it was empty by the time she visited, but that it left a "huge impression." She mentioned to him the stories of "babies being smacked against brick walls." Nothing more, just the babies. It choked them both up.

I presented this book to Mom on Mother's Day, 2002. At first she didn't understand. Then Betty said, "Jean, it's a book about you." She began to sob, silently at first, and then sniffling. "Thank you" was all she said to us as we shared her emotion. So in the end, this effort to record Mom's story for her grandkids became more – a statement to, as well as about, her – now, and ever after.

May 12, 2002
Springfield, Missouri

Dearest Mom,

Thank you for all you have done for us, including going to war. You have set a standard, through example, for compassion, grit, bravery, resiliency and unconditional love. We will forever be better for the life you have lived.

Love, Patrick and Todd

Postscript

Loss of husband and service to country were battles fought and won. Mom is waging her biggest battle now. She slides down a slippery Alzheimer's slope, leaving two-ton trucks, donuts and family behind, the latter clinging to precious remnants of her noble spirit.

Alzheimer's is a brutal enemy. It saps victims, loved ones and caregivers alike with a predictable timeline of destruction and devastation. It is a mean and relentless stalker of sanity that discriminates not between healthy and sick, haves and have-nots, Presidents and plebeians. Anger, frustration, and hopelessness dot the final landscape.

On Veteran's Day 2003, as Mom drifted deeper into her disease, I was asked to share her story at a Rotary Club weekly meeting, this one a tribute to veterans. Wife Betty dressed Mom in her only remaining formal wear, a bright red skirt-jacket ensemble, and set her at the head table with me. Attending veterans were asked to stand and receive our grateful recognition. With help, Mom stood to join them. I then read excerpts from this text, struggling at times with the emotion of the moment. I closed by presenting my mother-heroine, Jean Hogg Parnell.

The room rose as one, voices raised in tribute. Mom struggled to her feet, leaned into her audience, waved back and blew kisses. I shall never forget her final moment in the sun.

Tiny, fragile Mom is still at war. She serves with bravery and honor that befit her past.

Todd Parnell
July 8, 2005

116

Scrapbook

THE TOMAHAWK

The Tomahawk Strikes!

Vol. IV No. 8

CLUBMOBILE GROUP C

LONDON, July 20. (delayed) Clubmobile Group C left London this afternoon for a marshalling area. We will wait for available transportation and at that time we will sail from a Port of Embarkation for the continent.

The entire unit consists of Mr. Earl Monson, Group Superintendent and Kay Curtis, and thirty girls...

Mom in Paris surrounded by soldiers.

Mom's Timeline (1944 - 1945)

6/2/44	Mom leaves Springfield Mo. for Washington D.C.
6/17/44	Mom graduates from Red Cross Training Program
7/6/44	Mom receives "clearance" for transit to Europe
7/9/44	Mom's class to NYC
7/14/44	Board Queen Elizabeth for England
7/22/44	Arrive Greenoch, Scotland
7/23/44	Arrive London
8/1/44	Assignment to Southwest England
10/13/44	Group C to Heerleen, Holland
10/18/44	Mom leaves S.W. England to join Group C
11/19/44	Arrive Heerleen
11/26/44	Hotel shelled (Nederlandia Hotel)
12/28/44	Aachen, Germany (Bergebhof Hotel)
	Battle of the Bulge
	Serve troops in:
	- Stoleberg, Germany
	- Eschweiler, Germany
2/8/45	Kohlscheid, Germany
	(remainder of time in Germany except as indicated)
2/23/45	Troops crossed Ruhr River, take Jülich
2/25/45	Clubmobiles cross Ruhr to Jülich
3/1/45	Troops take München-Gladbach (home of Goebbels)
3/2/45	Clubmobiles serve troops in Müchen-Gladbach
3/2/45	Reach Rhine at Düsseldorf, don't cross
3/6/45	Clubmobiles serve troops at Neuss
3/8/45	Korschenbroich
3/28/45	Cross Rhine at Wesel, enter Friedrechsfeld
4/5/45	Weidenbruch
4/9/45	Steinheim
4/10/45	Cross Weser River at Hameln
4/13/45	Hildeshieme
4/16/45	Oschersleben
5/4/45	Harz Mountains
5/7/45	VE Day
5/8/45	Friedberg – arrive midnight after all day convoy
5/12/45	Bad Wildungen (Gen. Bradley, victory party)
5/17/45	Bad Nauheim
5/26/45	Frankfort
	Cannes, Paris (R&R)
7/12/45	Wiesbaden
9/18/45	Friedburg
11/16/45	Arrive NYC

The End